Fascism

CAMBRIDGE PERSPECTIVES IN HISTORY
Series editors: Richard Brown and David Smith

Fascism

Richard Thurlow
The University of Sheffield

CAMBRIDGE
UNIVERSITY PRESS

CAMBRIDGE UNIVERSITY PRESS
Cambridge, New York, Melbourne, Madrid, Cape Town, Singapore, São Paulo

Cambridge University Press
The Edinburgh Building, Cambridge CB2 8RU, UK

www.cambridge.org
Information on this title: www.cambridge.org/9780521598729

First published 1999
Third printing 2004

A catalogue record for this publication is available from the British Library

ISBN 978-0-521-59872-9 paperback

Transferred to digital printing 2008

Text design by Newton Harris Design Partnership

Acknowledgements
Cover, Private Collection/Bridgeman Art Library, London/New York; 8, Ullstein
Bilderdienst; 27, 44, 55, Hulton Getty Picture Collection Ltd; 31, Peter Newark's
Historical Pictures; 46, Centre for the Study of Cartoons and Caricature,
University of Kent, Canterbury; 53, Bilderdienst Süddeutscher Verlag; 65, AKG
Photo, London; 71, David King Collection; 87, Popperfoto.

The cover illustration shows Heinrich Himmler and his SS Council by Gianetto
Coppola. (We have been unable to trace the copyright holder of this painting
and would be grateful for any information that would enable us to do so.)

The publisher would like to thank Roger Griffin, Ruth Henig, Chris Clark and
Peter Neville for their contributions to the development of this book.

Contents

Contents

1 What is fascism?

'Fascism' is one of the most controversial political terms in modern history. The lack of a universally accepted definition for the term has meant that it has been applied to a wide variety of political contexts. For example, it can be deemed as only being applicable to Mussolini's regime in Italy between 1922 and 1943; as the 'highest stage of capitalism' in its most nakedly aggressive form by Marxist commentators; as a concept which can be applied to the form of government exercised in both Mussolini's Italy and Nazi Germany; as a type of paramilitary, nationalist movement which surfaced in many European countries during the inter-war period; or simply as an insulting term provoked by any display of authoritarian behaviour. There is also no common agreement as to whether its roots lie in the political right or left, or even if it had any kind of coherent, unified ideology or world view.

Interpretations of fascism

After Mussolini came to power in 1922 and subsequently created a Fascist dictatorship in Italy, he provoked a debate about what Fascism stood for. When Mussolini was asked what Fascism meant, he replied cryptically 'It is action'. But was fascism really a new phenomenon? The question of what fascism stood for has not yet been successfully resolved. A debate still rages in particular about whether the German variant of fascism, national socialism, or Nazism, can be accurately described as being fascist at all (see Table 1). Nazism, after all, involved a belief in biological determinism, especially the assumption that the Aryan race was superior to all others; it was also intensely anti-Semitic. Neither of these characteristics of German Nazism was a feature of Italian Fascism (at least, not until Mussolini's attempts to introduce anti-Jewish laws in 1938). If one

	Fascism	Nazism
Anti-communism	✓	✓
Extreme nationalism	✓	✓
Racial-superiority concept		✓
Anti-Semitism*		✓
Aggressive foreign policy	✓	✓

* Mussolini's later anti-Semitism can be dismissed as a feeble copy of the German model; anti-Semitism was not part of the original Fascist programme.

Table 1. A comparison between the ideological components of Fascism and Nazism.

takes the Italian version as a fascist model, it is therefore perhaps possible to argue that national socialism was not a truly fascist ideology. Indeed, many other fascist movements, such as Oswald Mosley's British Union of Fascists in Britain, tended to copy Mussolini's model of fascism rather than the German version. The problem is further complicated by Mussolini's opportunism and political compromises with the Italian establishment once in power, whereas Hitler was far more radical in his implementation of Nazi policies. Some historians, like Denis Mack Smith,[1] see little consistency and much opportunism in *Il Duce*'s ('the leader's') behaviour. Others argue that fascism was such a product of special national circumstances that it is dangerous to generalise about common patterns. To simplify matters in this book, 'Fascist' and 'Fascism' will be used to denote Mussolini's movement, and 'fascist' and 'fascism' those movements which followed the Italian *or* German models (see Glossary).

Fascism as a third force

One approach to the problem posed by the definition of fascism is to treat it as a revolutionary form of nationalism. According to this view, fascism can be seen as a kind of third force, lying somewhere between capitalism and communism, designed to create a new type of society (fascist movements commonly referred to the need for a national 'rebirth'). This definition covers two major inter-war fascist regimes, those of Fascist Italy and the German Third Reich, as well as a wide range of movements that were prevalent during both the inter-war and post-war periods which never achieved political power. If this definition is accepted, as it has been in this book, fascism can be seen as one of the most important political phenomena of the twentieth century. Indeed, one can go further and say that it is tempting to view fascism as the most distinctive new political idea of the twentieth century.

Although some of fascism's roots derive from both a cultural revolution and the political substrata of late nineteenth-century Europe, its primary importance stems from its meteoric rise and fall in the twentieth century, between 1922 and 1945. As a reactionary form of ultra-nationalism, fascism was important because although it was only in Italy (1922–43) and Germany (1933–45) that its proponents attained power, it had far-reaching effects: Hitler's attempt to transform and aggrandise Germany through the formation of a 'Thousand-year Reich' led to the establishment of a vast military empire, stretching from the Atlantic seaboard of France to the Ural Mountains in the USSR and from the North Cape in Norway to the Mediterranean Sea. The Second World War, a conflict provoked by Hitler's policies, ultimately caused the deaths of nearly 30 million Europeans, and perhaps 50 million people world-wide, and led to the division of Europe for nearly 50 years after 1945.

Theories of generic fascism

Interpretations which stress the common characteristics of fascist movements, as in this book, can be seen as stemming from a theory of generic fascism. Such theories assume that the similarities between fascist movements are more significant than the differences. They have been developed to explain the causes, structure, support or ideology of fascist movements or regimes. The most significant theories have stemmed from proponents of Marxist theories, from 'extremism of the centre', totalitarianism and modernisation theories, as well as those of Ernst Nolte and the 'new consensus' schools. These theories will each be discussed in turn.

Marxist theories of fascism

Marxist interpretations (see also Chapter 6) saw fascism as a repressive response of monopoly capitalism to the economic, political and social crisis caused by the First World War and the Bolshevik Revolution. Fascism was regarded as a form of reactionary political terrorism, manipulated by capitalist forces as their agent, whose function was to destroy the labour movement and all forms of democracy, thus ultimately leading to the dictatorship of capital. Stalin argued that fascism had now replaced imperialism as the 'highest stage of capitalism' before the latter's inevitable destruction by socialist revolution. Stalin also argued that the failure of reformist socialists to accept the communist leadership of revolutionary action against fascism/capitalism made them effectively 'social fascists'.

Although both inter- and post-war Marxists developed more sophisticated theories which differentiated between fascism, capitalism and the bourgeois state, Marxist theories remain unconvincing. The lack of supporting evidence for collaboration or collusion by governing elites with fascists, the assumption that all capitalists had the same outlook, the belief that fascism and capitalism had similar economic interests, the presence of anti-capitalist themes within fascism, and the failure of the 'united' and 'popular' fronts (see Chapter 6) to check fascist imperialism, all limit the plausibility of Marxist theories of fascism.

'Extremism of the centre'

In his book *Political man*, Seymour Martin Lipset[2] argued in favour of a non-Marxist, class-based theory of fascism. Lipset stated that fascism represented an 'extremism of the centre' – that is, the lower-middle-class and middle-class's reaction to political and economic crisis. While it is of some help in explaining the growth of Nazism, this theory understates the shift of constituency of the National Socialist German Workers' Party (*Nationalsozialistische Deutsche Arbeiterpartei*, or NSDAP) from being a relatively middle-class-based party in 1930 to one having a broader constituency with the deepening economic depression in 1932. Neither does it explain why Mussolini could become such a potent political force in Italy in 1922 on so narrow an electoral base, as the Fascists held only 38 of the 630 seats. Lipset does not emphasise the nature and appeal of 'agrarian Fascism' in Emilia-Romagna and Apulia (Italy) in 1922 and Schleswig-Holstein, East Prussia, Pomerania, Hanover and Mecklenburg (Germany) or the disproportionate success of Nazism in rural Protestant areas of Germany. The evidence that Lipset proposes, that it was generally members of the political liberal centre rather than traditional conservatives who became fascists, is also problematic, as liberals were alienated by the authoritarianism of fascism.

Totalitarianism

Whereas Marxist scholarship argued that capitalism and fascism were closely linked, Hannah Arendt[3] and Carl Friedrich[4], writing in the Cold War period, instead suggested that fascism and communism were similar in their political structures, linked by a common practice of 'totalitarianism'. Particular emphasis was placed on their seemingly corresponding power structures, the roles of their respective parties, the bureaucratic nature of the state under such regimes and their common use of terror. Arendt and Friedrich thus emphasised the parallels between the Nazi and Soviet states. However, such comparisons ignored the fundamental differences between public and private ownership of property in the two societies, as well as their radically opposed ideologies – in the case of communism based on class, in the case of fascism on race.

Modernisation theories

In part a development of the totalitarian thesis, some modernisation theories have suggested that fascism represented a 'developmental dictatorship', an alternative to the communist and liberal models of economic development – for example, A. J. Gregor[5] suggested that Fascist Italy became the model for post-1945 Third World economic development. Henry Ashby Turner[6] argued the opposite – that fascism was an anti-modernising force, citing Hitler's plans for the 'new order' which allegedly envisaged the de-urbanisation of much of eastern Europe, ethnic cleansing on a vast scale, the mass murder of Jews and the enslavement of the surviving Slav populations.

There is continuing debate over the process of modernisation, as well as enduring controversy regarding patterns of economic growth and social mobility, based as these patterns are on the interpretation of statistics in both Fascist Italy and Nazi Germany. It has been argued that Nazism swept away the authoritarian structure of imperial and Weimar Germany, creating social-mobility patterns which enabled the democratic, post-Nazi West Germany to achieve impressive rates of economic growth. Conversely, the extent to which Hitler modernised Germany has been called into question, given that the Nazis were responsible for the Holocaust, for the 'euthanasia' of those who were deemed by the Nazis to be 'without value', for anti-feminist policies and for provoking the Second World War, all of which can be said to have had more in common with medieval forms of barbarism than with modern conceptions of civilised behaviour.

Ernst Nolte and *Three faces of fascism*

The German philosopher-historian Ernst Nolte developed an influential, if much criticised, theory in his book *Three faces of fascism*.[7] Nolte argued that fascism was an 'epochal phenomenon' which dominated the 'era of the world wars' (1914–45). Fascism, he said, had various stages of development. The

French *Action Française* represented a backward link from early fascism to the European reactionary tradition, which developed in opposition to the radical social and political reforms of the French Revolution; Italian Fascism was the mature form of the phenomenon; and Nazism was 'radical fascism'. For Nolte, fascism has to be understood as an ideological counter-offensive against communist internationalism and also against the belief in reason and progress, as well as the questioning of tradition and authority, that had its modern roots in the eighteenth-century Enlightenment. Although Nolte regarded fascism as 'anti-Marxism', he said that its revolutionary style and mass politics were borrowed from its enemy. Nolte, more controversially, alleged that the concept and practices involved in the Holocaust also mirrored those of the USSR during Stalin's political purges of his imagined enemies of the 1930s.

Nolte failed to examine the economic and social background to the rise of fascism; his linking of the *Action Française* to the fascist tradition was misleading; and his philosophical discussion of fascism ignored some of those Enlightenment traditions which influenced fascist ideas. Nolte nevertheless succeeded in re-activating interest in the political styles and ideologies of fascist movements. Even though Nolte's descriptive approach (his study of the organisation and ideas of fascism) was not extensively copied, his stimulating ideas were an influence on the 'new consensus' study of the projected aims and Utopian beliefs of fascists.

The 'new consensus'

During the 1990s, new life was breathed into the debate on the interpretation of the concept of fascism. Several new definitions were suggested as 'ideal types' or abstract models – what Nolte called the 'fascist minimum'. Stanley Payne[8] expanded upon an earlier definition which emphasised that fascism was an 'anti-movement' which opposed all existing political forms and possessed a distinctive political style and organisation. According to Payne's theory, fascism's negations reflected its status as a late-comer; its attack on existing political ideologies and groups was a way of competing for political space.

Payne's new definition had been influenced by the theory of Roger Griffin,[9] who defined fascism as an ideology of 'populist ultra-nationalism' advocating 'national rebirth'. Griffin argued that at their deepest levels all forms of fascism contained a 'mythic core', which comprised a belief in the necessity of destroying existing political forms and the establishment of a 'new order' based on the 'new values' of the 'new fascist man'. These varied somewhat within different national contexts but could incorporate both the allegedly heroic, fearless ideals of an ancient Roman centurion (Mussolini's favourite analogy) and the materialistic, racial nationalism of Nazism, with its adulation of the supposedly 'superior' qualities of the mythical Aryan or Nordic man.

Griffin's emphasis on the 'positive' ideology of fascism (regarding the 'new world' that the fascists were striving to create) found parallels in the work of Roger Eatwell.[10] Eatwell's theories were also compatible with Payne's definition of fascism, as well as with the emphasis placed on the significance of the ideology of fascism in the earlier, controversial work of Zeev Sternhell.[11] Eatwell argued that as well as the reactionary, right-wing, mythical side of fascism, there were also rational, left-wing influences which emphasised the importance of state intervention and planning. According to Eatwell, fascism represented a series of syntheses (or a blending) of ideas from both right- and left-wing ideologies, which created a 'third way' between capitalism and communism and was based on national, rather than individual, interests. Sternhell's work on fascist ideology also suggested that fascism was 'neither right nor left' and that fascism as an idea originated in France (although most of his work was based on the left-wing roots of French and Italian fascism).

In assessing these interpretations, Griffin argued that the 'new consensus' school was more unified than divided. This view, however, is debatable: Sternhell, for example, believed that the racial determinism of Nazism prevents it from being classified as a form of fascism, while Eatwell pointed out that Griffin originally failed to recognise the significance of fascist syntheses and ignored fascist economics. Payne's continued emphasis on style and organisation as defining elements of fascism has also been criticised. Yet there are, as Griffin points out, still sufficient commonly agreed 'new consensus' elements to allow the construction of a model of generic fascism as a third force: the 'alternative revolution'.

Fascism as an 'alternative revolution'

Fascism developed as a new political force in the aftermath of the First World War. It was a form of revolutionary nationalism, in that its proponents wished to rebuild the shattered fabric of the nation states of Europe and reverse the political, social and economic devastation caused by the war, a project which, in their eyes, was being threatened by the consequences of the Bolshevik Revolution. The fascist vision desired the creation of a new world 'fit for heroes' and the destruction of both the old order and the threat posed by revolutionary communism. Fascism attacked decadence and liberalism and exalted 'heroic' values and elitism. As a political late-comer, it created political space for itself by opposing all other political forms. Furthermore, the different cultural traditions of the European nations meant that fascism, as a revolutionary form of nationalism, developed a greater variety of beliefs and programmes than most other political ideas.

Fascism developed from both ends of the political spectrum. The deepest roots of Italian Fascism were in left-wing, national syndicalism – a form of socialism which believed in the ownership and control of industry by the workers (Mussolini was a revolutionary socialist until 1915). Conversely, Nazism evolved from the German political right, advocating extreme anti-Semitism and racial nationalism. What linked the two movements was a shared hostility to the threat of communist revolution, a belief in the necessity of overthrowing the existing political structure by revolutionary means, and the desired creation of a 'new order' based on national cultural myths. Mussolini, for example, wanted to build a new Roman empire which would endow the Italian 'new fascist man' with the values of both the ancient centurion and modern technology. Nazism similarly envisaged the creation of a social racial hierarchy in which, by positive discrimination, 'Aryan' Germans would obtain living space (*Lebensraum*) at the expense of 'lesser races'; those deemed to be 'inferior', such as Slavs, were to be denied living resources, while 'asocial' groups, such as the Jews, Gypsies, homosexuals, mentally and physically impaired and senile people, were to be 'eradicated'. These Utopian visions or 'dystopian nightmares' both foresaw a transformation of the nature of humans. Although there were significant differences between Italian Fascism and German Nazism – most notably over such ideological issues as the corporate state, anti-Semitism and racial nationalism – the basic structure of the mythical core of both Fascism and Nazism made them part of the same political family tree.

What differentiated the Italian Fascist Party (*Partito Nazionale Fascista*, or PNF) and the NSDAP from other forms of fascism was their political success. Yet in order to obtain power, both forms initially had to enter coalition governments; only Hitler was to escape fully from the constraints imposed by the need to co-operate with the components of the existing political structure and national establishment. Whereas it took Hitler only four months to obtain complete power through the Enabling Act in 1933, it took nearly seven years (from 1922 to 1929) for Mussolini to destroy all credible opposition to him. With the death of President Paul von Hindenburg in 1934, Hitler was able to combine the posts of president and chancellor of Germany. As *Führer* ('leader'), to whom soldiers and officials swore a personal oath of loyalty, he was responsible to no higher authority, and his pre-eminent personal position during the Third Reich was unchallenged until his suicide in his Berlin bunker in 1945. Mussolini, on the other hand, was responsible for his actions to King Victor Emmanuel III, who, although backing Mussolini during the various crises of his premiership – particularly the Matteotti crisis of 1924 – nevertheless removed Mussolini from power in 1943 when it was obvious that the war was lost.

Thus Hitler rapidly escaped from the constraints imposed on him by conservative interests in Germany, while Mussolini was forced to compromise with the Italian establishment. The Nazi state became increasingly radical as the restraints on Hitler's personal authority lessened and the influence of the NSDAP and the *Schutzstaffel* (SS) grew. Mussolini's Italy, on the other hand, reflecting both its actual status as a second-class power and the *Duce*'s reluctance to challenge the conservative establishment, saw a marked discrepancy between the bombastic rhetoric of Fascism and political reality. Mussolini's compromises, as well as the subordination of the PNF to the state, meant that his regime became increasingly conservative. Fascism can therefore be said to have come to mean 'stillborn revolution' in Italy and 'racial revolution' in Nazi Germany.

The various stages of development of fascism reflected the power relationships within and between the fascist states. During the 1920s, for example, the Italian PNF was the model for all aspiring fascist parties and Mussolini was admired by

Adolf Hitler and Benito Mussolini together in Munich in 1937. What characteristics did Fascism and Nazism have in common?

Hitler. Although he established the 'Fascist International' in 1934, in an attempt to influence and control fascist movements in other countries, and funded several foreign fascist movements, including Sir Oswald Mosley's British Union of Fascists, Mussolini rapidly became Hitler's client. Mussolini was envious of Hitler's success in Germany, and although he successfully opposed a Nazi rising in Austria in 1934 following the murder of the Austrian chancellor, Engelbert Dollfuss, the League of Nations' sanctions against Italy after the invasion of Abyssinia in 1935 forced him to accept Hitler as an ally. The 'brutal friendship' proved a one-sided relationship, however, as Mussolini was an unreliable ally whose actions hindered rather than helped Nazi Germany during the Second World War. Mussolini's deposition and imprisonment in 1943 led Hitler to rescue him and install him as a vassal ruler in the Italian Social Republic from 1943 to 1945, when Mussolini tried, unsuccessfully, to revert to his roots and establish a form of Fascist syndicalism.

Only in Fascist Italy and Nazi Germany was the 'fascist revolution' successful. Apart from limited collaboration during the later stages of the war with the Arrow Cross Party in Hungary and the Iron Guard in Romania, elsewhere conservatives had no need to make alliances with weak fascist movements. Indeed, fascist movements were generally suppressed by the state, and as a result of their marginalisation many fascist parties retained their revolutionary spirit, even when they had some political influence. Only as a potential 'fifth column' – hostile infiltrators of the state – in Norway, The Netherlands and France in 1940 (and the reality of this happening was much exaggerated by contemporaries) did they acquire a certain notoriety, but Hitler usually ignored fascist attempts to grab a share of power in their native countries through collaborating with him.

The fascist Axis powers (Germany and Italy) and their alliance with Japan during the Second World War reflected the dominance of Nazism in Europe, for Germany was very much the leading power. As a result, the 'alternative revolution' of fascism can be said to have reflected to some extent the Nazi dystopian fantasy of 'racial revolution' during the Second World War. In the event, only the destructive preparatory stage of the project was implemented: as a result of the Holocaust of European Jewry, the savage butchery of soldiers and civilians on the Eastern Front, and the 'ethnic cleansing' and 'racial war' inherent in Operation Barbarossa (the invasion of the USSR from 1941), at least 30 million Europeans were killed. Such was the price of radical fascism's 'alternative revolution'.

What is fascism?

1.1 An anti-generic interpretation

First of all, Fascism is not a generic concept. The word *fascismo* has no meaning beyond Italy. Yet it was applied from the beginning to the movements that arose in other nations, movements whose fate it was to be interpreted in terms of Mussolini's organisation. Such parties presumably corresponded to foreign 'models', first the Blackshirts and later the Nazis. 'They claim that we are fascists, but they know that this is a lie', protested Jacques Doriot, the leader of the Parti Populaire Français, in 1937. 'We do not think that the regime of Hitler can be fitted into our country'. Such men, however, could no more get rid of the word in their time than the historian can be rid of it today.

Source: Gilbert Allardyce, 'What fascism is not: thoughts on the deflation of a concept', *American Historical Review*, vol. 84 (1979), p. 370

1.2 A Marxist interpretation

Born in the womb of bourgeois democracy, fascism in the eyes of the capitalists is a means of saving capitalism from collapse. It is only for the purpose of deceiving and disarming the workers that social democracy denies the fascistisation of bourgeois democratic countries and the countries of the fascist dictatorship.

Source: extract from the plenum on fascism, the Communist International, December 1933, quoted in R. Griffin (ed.), *Fascism: a reader*, Oxford, 1995, p. 263

1.3 A 'new consensus' interpretation

If these fundamental characteristics are to be synthesised into a more succinct definition, fascism may be defined as 'a form of revolutionary ultra-nationalism for national rebirth that is based on a primarily vitalist philosophy, is structured on extreme elitism, mass mobilisation, and the *Führerprinzip* [leader principle], positively values violence as end as well as means and tends to normalise war and/or the military virtues'.

Source: Stanley Payne, *A history of fascism, 1914–45*, London, 1995, p. 14

1.4 Another 'new consensus' interpretation

Notwithstanding some genuine differences, I believe that time will show that in the context of the debate over fascism as a whole, what our ideal types have in common is more significant than what separates them. A promising sign of this is that some specialists are demonstrating how the new paradigm can be applied to studying particular fascist phenomena with encouraging empirical results.

Source: R. Griffin, *International fascism*, London, 1998, p. 15

1 What differences of interpretation of fascism are displayed by each of these sources?

2 In what ways are the Marxist interpretations of fascism (1.2) different from those of the 'new consensus' historians (1.3 and 1.4)?

3 Using these sources, why do you think that historians find it difficult to dispense with the concept of fascism?

4 Do you agree with 1.1 that fascism is not a generic concept?

5 What are the main features of fascism according to 1.3?

Notes and references

1 Denis Mack Smith, *Mussolini*, London, 1981.

2 Seymour Martin Lipset, *Political man*, London, 1983.

3 Hannah Arendt, *The origins of totalitarianism*, New York, 1951.

4 Carl Friedrich, *Totalitarianism*, London, 1954.

5 A. J. Gregor, 'Fascism and modernisation', *World Politics*, vol. 26 (1974).

6 Henry Ashby Turner, 'Fascism and modernisation', *World Politics*, vol. 24 (1972).

7 Ernst Nolte, *Three faces of fascism*, New York, 1969.

8 Stanley Payne, *A history of fascism, 1914–45*, London, 1995.

9 Roger Griffin, *The nature of fascism*, London, 1991, and *Fascism: a reader*, Oxford, 1995.

10 Roger Eatwell, *Fascism*, London, 1995.

11 Zeev Sternhell, *Neither right nor left: fascist ideology in France*, Berkeley, 1986.

2 The origins of fascism

Fascism developed from the destruction caused by the First World War. Its origins, however, can be traced to the intellectual revolt against liberalism in Europe at the end of the nineteenth century on the part of those who rejected the humanism of the Enlightenment and the 'ideas of 1789'. Yet while there was a revolutionary reaction against the ideals of the French Revolution (focused on liberty, equality and fraternity) before 1914, it was the First World War which was the real catalyst for the emergence of fascism. The war swept away the Hohenzollern, Habsburg and Romanov dynasties in Germany, Austria-Hungary and Russia respectively, sharpened class-consciousness, increased ethnic tensions and severely weakened the social fabric of many nations. Fascism was also the result of a reaction on the part of the middle classes against the perceived communist threat created by the Bolshevik Revolution in 1917.

Fascism was the most extreme reaction to this post-war political, social and national crisis. It was a movement which was opposed to the 'decadence' of existing politics and aimed to create a so-called 'new order' based on the idea of national 'rebirth' and renewal which was so strong in Nazi ideology. Yet the First World War also had a positive significance for the rise of fascism. The survivors of the 'lost generation' (the soldiers who had fought in the First World War), the 'trenchocracy', became embittered when the 'homes fit for heroes to live in' (as Britain's prime minister, David Lloyd George, eloquently promised) failed to materialise, and disillusioned veterans became attracted to the direct-action approach of fascist paramilitary organisations. The increased influence of the state, which assumed greater powers through massive orders for munitions and the control of consumption in many combatant nations, was to influence fascist theory and practice.

The deepest roots of fascism

The debate on the origins of fascism

The debate on the origins of fascism is as contentious as that on its nature. It focuses on the central question of the importance of the First World War in the emergence of fascism. Although it would be difficult to explain the sudden appearance of fascism without reference to the war's devastating impact on Europe, some historians have given prominence to longer-term causes. Four broad positions on the origins of fascism can be identified.

1 Those who stress the importance of ideology in the rise of fascism point to fascism's immediate roots in the revolt of some against the eighteenth-century Enlightenment, with its emphasis on rational thought and individual liberty.

2 Those who see cultural discontentment as deriving from the rapid pace of change associated with industrialisation and modernisation. This, they argue, triggered an anxiety which led some people to fascism.

3 A third group identifies deeper roots of fascism, in particular the existence in many German states from the time of the Protestant theologian Martin Luther (1483–1546) of extreme racial nationalism and anti-Semitism. Influential anti-Semites like Luther, and later the German philosopher Johann Gottlieb Fichte (1762–1814), regarded Jewish people as being 'alien' and 'un-German'. This strain of anti-Semitic prejudice, as well as disappointed expectations with regard to Germany's position in Europe on the part of extreme German nationalists after 1870, can be seen to have had a direct influence on Hitler.

4 In Italy, anti-Semitism was not a significant factor, but disappointed aspirations after the unification of the country in 1870 as a result of the failure of Italian imperialism in Africa and continuing social unrest alienated Italian nationalists and contributed to the rise of Fascism. This deep resentment reinforced the anger of Italians, who felt cheated by the 1919 peace settlement which failed to allow Italy to acquire Trieste and the Dalmatian coast, just as Germans felt humiliated by the terms of the Treaty of Versailles.

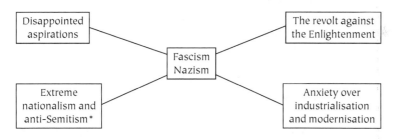

* Germany only

Table 2. The origins of fascism.

The ideological components of fascism

The difficulty with these views on fascism's roots stems from the fact that fascism did not exist before 1919. *Fascio* is an Italian word, meaning 'band', 'union' or 'league', which had traditionally been used to refer to left-wing populist movements before Mussolini used the term more specifically. It is only with the advantage of hindsight that certain events and influences dating from before 1914 can be seen as significant with regard to the origins of fascism (and even so, they are of minor importance). The national syndicalist movements on the left and the Italian Nationalist Association on the right of Italian politics were only small, extremist organisations by 1910. Although they would later provide supporters of the Italian PNF and would influence its thinking, they were politically marginal in pre-war Italy. Similarly, anti-Semitic parties and radical-right populism obtained only peripheral political representation in Bismarckian and Wilhelmine Germany.

While fascism undoubtedly owed much to a simplified form of the nineteenth-century revolt against rationalism, the impact of the latter on fascism needs careful analysis. It is absurd to blame philosophers, psychologists or sociologists, like the German philosopher Friedrich Wilhelm Nietzsche (1844–1900), the Italian political philosopher Vilfredo Pareto (1848–1923), the Italian political theorist Gaetano Mosca (1858–1941), the French philosopher Georges Sorel (1847–1922), the Austrian psychiatrist Sigmund Freud (1865–1939) or the French psychologist Gustave Le Bon (1841–1931), for having sown the seeds of fascism because the fascists misinterpreted their work. The Nazis misrepresented the ideas of the philosopher Nietzsche, for example, who put forward the concept of the Aryan *Übermensch* ('superman') but was completely apolitical and would have loathed the idea of the Nazi 'folk community', based as it was on racial criteria. In a similar fashion, Italian Fascists transformed Sorel's belief that general strikes could be used to achieve revolution into their own brand of anti-leftist nationalism. And the 'elite theorists' Mosca and Pareto, who had little faith in the political role of the masses, would have been shocked by the brutal behaviour of fascist leaders. German sociologist and political economist Max Weber's (1864–1920) sociological theory of charismatic leadership was also significant, but he would hardly have condoned the manic 'charisma' of Hitler or Mussolini. Le Bon's theory about the manipulation of crowds, put forward at the end of the nineteenth century, can in some respects be said to have much in common with modern advertising, with its emphasis on crude slogans and repetition; it is known to have influenced Mussolini and possibly Hitler as well. Fascist ideology was thus a ragbag of different ideas and concepts which were invariably distortions of the original theories that inspired them.

One thing above all is certain: fascism represented a clear rejection of what the French philosopher Jean Jacques Rousseau (1712–78) had said in the eighteenth century before the outbreak of the French Revolution (and he is recognised as

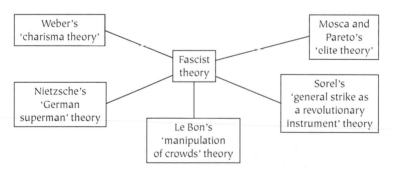

Table 3. The intellectual background of fascism.

having had a significant influence on it). Rousseau believed that humankind was not inherently evil and that ordinary people could be motivated to bring about change. Fascists, on the other hand, were contemptuous of the masses and sought transformation through strong, authoritarian and often brutal leadership.

Although fascism's ideology demonstrates considerable backward linkages to many political, economic, social and intellectual influences before 1914, it is important to remember how marginal and tenuous most of these were.

The impact of the First World War

The impact of hostilities transformed the fringe subculture of fascism into a virulent political form in inter-war Europe. The First World War destroyed the pre-1914 world. A whole generation of young men lost their lives in the trenches of the Western Front in such battles of attrition as the Somme (1916). Over 10 million Europeans died in the carnage. Unlike during the Second World War, the victims were mostly front-line soldiers and not civilians. Indeed, part of the cult of the 'lost generation' was the view that the cream of European youth had been destroyed in the futile slaughter, while politicians and civilians tried, as expressed by the American phrase, to 'return to normalcy'.

In reality, the First World War smashed the political structure of Europe, sweeping away the old ruling order. Those who remained were unable to re-create the institutions and trading networks which had facilitated the relatively smooth functioning of the nineteenth-century international economy and had led to the cessation of major international incidences of warfare since 1815, when the Congress of Vienna had settled the boundaries of Europe in the aftermath of the Battle of Waterloo. During the First World War, European states had been forced to promote organised capitalism in order to maximise production for the war effort; in so doing they had unleashed the powerful forces of industrial and political invention, innovation and modernisation.

While the war had undermined the pre-1914 social fabric of some parts of Europe, it had also created new methods of brutalising society which were to be developed by the Nazis. For, as Stanley Payne[1] pointed out, the Nazis did not 'invent' genocide. Between 1915 and 1923, for example, nearly 1 million Armenians were massacred by the Turks in a prototypical instance of genocide. Such brutal actions contributed to the overall sense of social and political alienation and desensitisation which resulted from the First World War.

The political response to the First World War

Politicians internationally were divided as to how they should respond to the cessation of hostilities in 1918. Britain and France wanted to punish their German enemy severely: to 'hang the Kaiser' and to 'squeeze Germany until the pips squeak'. Many Germans tried to pretend that their country had not been defeated, laying the foundation for the subsequent Nazi myth of the 'stab in the back' by asserting that civilian unrest at home had turned a potential German military victory into defeat.

The League of Nations

The decisive entry of the USA into the war on the side of Britain and France in April 1917 led to a brave attempt to set up a new international order, enforced by the League of Nations, based on President Woodrow Wilson's 'Fourteen Points'. The League was intended to defuse international tensions and end secret forms of diplomacy. Wilson's political idealism was unfortunately not shared by the US Senate, which refused to ratify the peace treaties or the Versailles settlement, which provided for the establishment of the League of Nations, a decision which ultimately led to the withdrawal of the world's foremost economic power into political isolation during the inter-war period. The non-participation of the USA fatally weakened the League of Nations from the outset and destroyed whatever chance there may have been of effective and disinterested international co-operation in avoiding or ameliorating international political conflicts.

The Bolshevik Revolution and the economic blockade

The fact that the victors fell out with each other and that the losers – although forced to accept defeat – were dissatisfied with the victors' attempt to destroy permanently their former power and status meant that the peace process was flawed from the start and undermined the restoration of normality to international relations.

The post-war crisis was made worse by two further factors: the Bolshevik Revolution of October 1917 and the prolongation of the economic blockade on the defeated powers until they had signed the peace treaties of 1919–20. The Bolshevik Revolution not only caused the withdrawal of Russia from the war but also raised the threat that revolutionary fervour would spread to the rest of Europe, which Lenin believed Bolshevik survival depended on because Soviet Russia could not survive in a hostile world. While his belief proved delusory in the long run, and the Stalinist USSR was to retreat to the position of 'socialism in one country', the collapse of the great imperial dynasties and political structures of central and eastern Europe between 1917 and 1918, allied to the economic and social impact of the blockade of these countries, created conditions which maximised the fear of the threat of the spread of communist revolution in the aftermath of the First World War. The fragility of the new democracies of central Europe, like Austria and Hungary, similarly contributed to this fear.

The emergence of fascism

It was the above combination of political, social and economic circumstances that encouraged the development of the conditions which ultimately led to the emergence of fascism. Although Italy was the only nation to become a Fascist state during the 1920s, proto-fascist movements emerged in many European nations as a result of the chaotic conditions after 1918. The emergence of fascism represented for the most part the defensive reaction of those who militantly opposed communism and wished to fill the political void created by the collapse of the old order with a non-communist alternative.

The first imperative was to crush communist attempts to seize power, as in the case of Béla Kun's revolution in Hungary, the Spartacist revolt led by Rosa Luxemburg and Karl Liebknecht in Berlin and the Socialist Bavarian Republic in Germany in 1919.

The emergence of the 'White Guards'

The emergence of vigilante groups of demobilised soldiers organised by former officers became the fulcrum of opposition to the westward spread of the Bolshevik Revolution, as was seen in the formation of the *Freikorps* in Germany, the *arditi* and *Fascio di Combattimento* in Italy and the Men of Szeged in Hungary. The 'White Guards', as these groups were also generically called by the Marxists, instigated a programme of counter-violence and terror against incidences of left-wing revolutionary activity in Europe. Proto-fascists, and later the 'true' fascists, can therefore not only be said to have been brutalised by the war experience but also to have copied the violent activities of left-wing revolutionaries for counter-revolutionary purposes. In Poland alone, and then only with the help of the French, did the regular army see off the communist threat (the Red army being repulsed before the gates of Warsaw). For the most part, these 'private armies' lacked a coherent ideology, being mainly battalions of volunteers who provided violent political resistance to communism in the vacuum caused by the collapse of state power. It was the linking of the pre-1914 ultra-nationalist political and cultural undercurrents with such examples of post-war paramilitary activism which led to the emergence of fascism.

If communism, in Lenin's words, was 'electrification plus soviet power', fascism originated in the cult of the 'heroic elite', allied to anti-communist political thuggery. In its various guises it rapidly developed a specific nationalist ideology which was as opposed to the discredited old order as it was to communism. It was therefore opposed to the re-establishment of the old elites in positions of power, which explains why radical-right populism and fascist-style movements were less than successful in eastern and central Europe, regions in which the conditions suitable for their growth were perhaps otherwise the most developed. In Romania, Poland and Hungary military and authoritarian right-wing dictatorships rapidly replaced the fledgling democracies created in 1918, which, apart from that in Czechoslovakia, were unable to cope with the combination of economic depression and the threat of communism. Most of these states either suppressed fascists and members of the radical right or tolerated them as political 'safety valves' in instances where, as in Hungary, much of the orthodox left had been outlawed. Sometimes these policies were run consecutively: in Romania, for example, King Carol II's government ordered the shooting of the fascist leader Corneliu Codreanu in 1938 'while he was trying to escape'; later, after having been forced to co-operate with Hitler, the Romanian prime minister – effectively a military dictator – Ion Antonescu for a time found it expedient to work with the fascist Iron Guard formed by Codreanu.

Why fascism emerged in post-war Europe

Fascism can therefore be said to have developed as a response to the crisis created by the First World War. As a concept, fascism owed its origins to the pronouncements of the Comintern (the Communist International formed in 1919 to promote revolutionary Marxism) which, during the early 1920s, linked the anti-communist, counter-revolutionary activities of the 'White Guards' to the rapid rise of Italian Fascism.

But what were the main factors which contributed to the emergence of fascism after 1918? As we have discussed, of central significance was the crisis created by the First World War, which destabilised the political and economic structure of many European countries. This was compounded by the impact of the Bolshevik Revolution and the resistance to its expansion to eastern and central Europe by many social elites, military officers and demobilised soldiers. Fascism also needed to find a political space in which to develop, and this depended on the extent to which either the state apparatus of power, or law and order, collapsed, and how well the authorities coped with the real or imagined threat of revolution.

Fascism was as opposed to the 'decadence' of inter-war society as it was to the Bolshevik Revolution, being anti-conservative, anti-liberal, anti-socialist and anti-parliamentarian. Although it upheld the principle of private property, there were strong anti-capitalist elements in early fascism. The corporate state, with the interests of producers, workers, consumers and the government theoretically being equally represented, was often seen by early fascists as being a more just system of economic organisation than the free market and capitalist control could be subordinated to the national interest. Indeed, the strong syndicalist influence on early Italian Fascism advocated workers' control of productive industry. Such 'anti-movements' also needed positive political ideas, which they usually borrowed from the nineteenth-century intellectual revolt against the ideals of the French Revolution and nineteenth-century liberalism, and which they combined with a virulent form of ultra-nationalism and a Utopian vision of a modernised, united society to form an independent, fascist-style movement. It was in Italy and Germany that these ingredients were given political direction by the emergence of movements which can be described as fascist.

As well as the political and national structural problems caused by the war, specific economic and social factors worsened the crisis. The problem of the demobilisation of their armies created various crises of adjustment in many European states. Inflation and unemployment led many to become disillusioned and despairing, and the feeling of frustrated expectations was made worse by the non-materialisation of wartime promises of 'homes fit for heroes to live in', more land for agricultural labourers, universal suffrage and an extension of social ownership of property. Many regarded the sacrifices of the Great War as having been in vain, as plans for radical reform were put on ice, while the communist revolution led to chaos, famine, terror and civil war in many countries. Fascism was not the only response to the disillusionment created by the First World War and its immediate aftermath: communism, socialism, pacifism, anarchism and political Catholicism attracted many of those who had failed to readjust to the peacetime situation and who blamed political democracy for the failure of their countries to recover from the devastating effects of the war.

Fascism: the 'third way'?

As a so-called 'third way' between capitalism and communism, fascism proved a Utopian delusion. Yet its mythical propaganda – that dynamic activism would provide the impetus to solve the political, economic and social crisis of the inter-war years – attracted many. It even had a degree of plausibility, given the failure of liberal democracy in many countries and the social cost of full employment in the Soviet Union.

Yet fascism would be an even greater failure. It never had any electoral appeal in western Europe outside Germany and Italy. Its policies of the racist and political persecution of 'undesirable' social elements and its willingness to wage war in the furtherance of its aims would unite its enemies, whose resistance to fascism would ultimately lead to the collapse of the fascist delusion. Ironically, fascism would finally be defeated by an alliance between Soviet communism and Anglo-American liberal democracy.

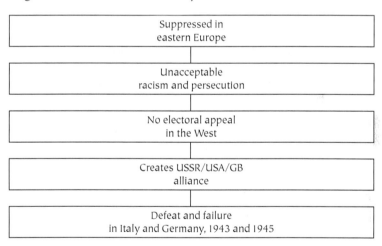

Table 4. The failure of fascism.

The post-war dissatisfaction of the 'lost generation'

2.1 A British spokesman for the 'lost generation'

Chesterton is more than a brilliant and incisive writer. He is a living symbol of the lost generation which has found itself again. More than any writer of his time, he expresses in dynamic and passionate prose the resurgent soul of the war generation . . .
Supremely characteristic of the Englishman of 1914, he could find no home but Fascism
. . . Chesterton expresses their fierce disgust and their cold anger in the bitterness of a thousand betrayals. He recaptures also the rapturous spirit of 1914 in their undying march to greater heights and mightier service to the land they love.

Source: preface by Sir Oswald Mosley to A. K. Chesterton, *Creed of a fascist revolutionary*, London, 1934, p. 3

2.2 The origins of the German *Freikorps*

They were the troublemakers in their companies. War had not yet demobbed them. The war had formed them, causing their most secret obsessions to break through the surface and sparkle in the dark. It had given their life a meaning and sanctified their sense of duty. They were unruly, untamed. Cast out of the world of bourgeois norms, they had not returned to their regiments, but formed small groups to look for their own front to defend . . . They had seen through the fraud of the peace settlement, and wanted no part in it. They wanted no part of the political order which people were trying to make them digest with slippery promises. They had stayed under arms out of an unwavering instinct.

Source: Ernst von Saloman, *Die Geächteten* ['The outcasts'], Berlin, 1930, p. 63. Translated by Roger Griffin, in R. Griffin (ed.), *Fascism: a reader*, Oxford, 1995, p. 110

1 What do these sources tell us about the influence of the First World War on the fascist mentality?

2 In what ways do these sources criticise the alleged 'decadence' of 'bourgeois norms'?

3 What do these sources tell us about the 'lost generation's' alienation from contemporary inter-war society?

4 What do these sources tell us about why fascism should have developed as a distinctive new political movement after the First World War?

Notes and references

1 Stanley Payne, *A history of fascism, 1914–45*, London, 1995.

3 Mussolini and Italian Fascism

Although fascism, in the sense of a revolutionary, populist brand of nationalism, was a general European phenomenon of the inter-war period, it was spawned in Italy. The term *'fascio'* had first been applied to the small radical groups which had emerged in nineteenth-century Italy. *'Fascio'* is derived from the Latin word *fasces*, which referred both to a bundle of sticks with protruding axeheads tied together and to a symbol of authority which was carried by a minor Roman official who preceded magistrates in procession in the streets of ancient Rome. The rods represented punishment; the axe, execution. It became an apt symbol for Fascism after it had identified itself with both the total power of the state and Italy's Roman legacy.

The first successful fascist movement may have developed in Italy, but it only partially transformed the Italian state and society and was rapidly overtaken as a model for other fascist regimes by Nazism in the 1930s. The many political and cultural currents which influenced the formation of Fascism, class and regional divisions in Italian society, lack of natural resources and difficulties in projecting a revolutionary national identity were all serious weaknesses which limited Mussolini's options. Yet Mussolini remained in power from 1922 to 1943 before becoming leader of the Italian Social Republic from 1943 to 1945, making him the longest-serving Italian leader of the twentieth century. While political realities necessitated a succession of compromises, it was not surprising that opportunism, as much as ideology, influenced the emergence of the Fascist state. The Fascist regime proved more conservative than radical, especially in its economic and social policy. Indeed, the only constant feature of Italian Fascism was the personality cult of *'Il Duce'* ('the leader'), as 'Mussolinism' became the most pronounced characteristic of the Fascist state.

In retrospect, it can be said that Fascism failed to create either a new Italy or a 'new man'. Italians did not believe in the Fascist slogan of 'Believe, obey, fight' and they became increasingly sceptical of the claim 'The *Duce* is always right'. In spite of the scars induced by the civil war between 1943 and 1945, Fascism left only a minor legacy, despite the longevity of Mussolini's rule. The Fascist concordat with the papacy, the codification of the legal system, the building of the *autostrada* (motorways), corporatism, the draining of the Pontine Marshes and relative self-sufficiency in food production were the main lasting political and economic achievements of Fascism. The national obsession with organised sport, *'nostalgia l'avvenire'* (nostalgia for the Fascist tradition) and a neo-Fascist-minority political tradition organised around the MSI (*Movimenti Sociale Italiano*), craving the political authority and leadership of a Mussolini figure, were also legacies of the Fascist era.

The origins of Fascism

The formal birth of Fascism is usually dated from Mussolini's meeting with the 'Fascists of the first hour' at the Piazza San Sepolcro, Milan, in March 1919. Before then, however, the social elements which later blended into Fascism had already been involved in the 'radiant days of May' in 1915, when the populist campaign of the interventionists clamoured for Italian participation in the First World War. The *Fasci di Azione Rivoluzionaria* were Mussolini's left-wing interventionists, a group of national syndicalists and former socialists who advocated 'revolutionary war' on the side of the 'progressive' Entente powers, Britain and France. War, they believed, would arouse national feeling among the masses, aid the modernisation and reorganisation of the economy and lead to revolutionary change. The left-wing interventionists joined forces with the extreme-right-wing elitist and imperialist Italian Nationalist Association (*Alleanza Nazionale*) which led the propaganda campaign to enter the war. The link between the two groups was their joint demand for intervention in the war and their belief that Italy was a 'proletarian nation' that had been condemned by the international political system to an inferior status and was being exploited by the other powers. Filippo Marinetti's Futurist movement, which advocated the radical renewal of Italian culture and society and worshipped technology and all things modern, was also an important component in the informal interventionist alliance and early Fascism. Similarly, the Romantic poet Gabriele D'Annunzio loudly proclaimed interventionism in 1915; although never a Fascist, his occupation of Fiume from 1919 to 1920 (to assert Italy's claim to the Dalmatian port in defiance of the terms of the Treaty of Versailles which declared it a free city) was to be an important influence on the propaganda, mass politics and theatrical style of Mussolini's Italy.

The main difference between the disaffected groups who agitated for change in 1915 and 1919 was the addition of the battle-hardened *arditi* (crack troops of the Italian Army) to the fascist groups (*Fasci di Combattimento*), demobilised officers who found it difficult to adjust to conditions in post-war Italy, the collapse of state authority and the threat of revolutionary socialism. Fascism would reflect all these different influences; the general pattern of political events would see a decline in the influence of left-wing syndicalism and corporatism and an increase in the significance of the authoritarian, nationalist right as Mussolini compromised with the Italian establishment (that is, until he attempted to revert to his radical roots in the final days of the Italian Social Republic).

The deeper roots of Italian Fascism

While Italian Fascism can be said to have been a product of the First World War, its deepest roots reflected nationalist dissatisfaction with the less than glorious history of the new Italian state. Italy was a creation of the 1860s (and was finally unified in 1870), formed largely as a result of the efforts of the *Risorgimento*, or national independence movement, which demanded the establishment of an independent Italian state (although there was considerable division about whether this state should take a republican form, as advocated by the great nationalist Giuseppe Mazzini, or a monarchical one). The process of unification was masterminded by Count Cavour, the prime minister of Piedmont until 1861 and the instigator of the successful war of 1859 against Austria. Cavour was in an uneasy alliance with the republican Giuseppe Garibaldi, whose thousand Redshirts conquered the largest Italian kingdom of Naples in 1860. Italy's origins as a nation symbolised the weakness of the new state, a divided nation which needed outside assistance in order to be politically viable.

The hopes of Italian patriots for their nation were to be continually frustrated. The new state was split by geography, politics and religion. Italy was a dual economy, with a relatively advanced, but small, industrial sector in the north and a backward, stagnant, rural economy in the south, where there were high rates of illiteracy, malaria and underemployment. The nation developed more in the image of the liberal Cavour than the revolutionary populist Garibaldi and was governed by a small elite which manipulated a parliament elected on a narrow franchise. Italy's governments were unstable and short-lived coalitions, hence the anti-parliamentarianism of the Fascists. Italy was also weakened because the papacy refused to co-operate with the new state (the Vatican objected to its loss of the Papal States which occurred when the Italian nation was created). These internal problems were increased when Italy failed to gain its imperialist 'place in the sun' after its defeat by the Abyssinians (Ethiopians) at the Battle of Adowa (1896), a humiliation which was only partly redeemed by the annexation of a few coastal oases following the Italo-Turkish War (1911–12). Italy became increasingly riven by social conflict and weak government. Neither state repression by Francesco Crispi and Luigi Pelloux during the 1890s nor the social-appeasement policy of Giovanni Giolitti's governments before the First World War were successful in diminishing agrarian unrest and industrial strife.

The impact of the First World War on Italian society

The rise of Fascism resulted primarily from the impact of the First World War on Italian society. Italy's failure to acquire all the territory demanded by the interventionists in the peace settlement, particularly with regard to Fiume and the Dalmatian coast, led to resentment amongst nationalists, who railed against the 'mutilated peace'. The post-war settlement partly reflected the less than effective contribution that the Italians had made to the victory of the Entente powers. The Italian army's appalling treatment of its peasant conscripts, low morale among the soldiers and the generals' obsession with an inappropriate offensive military strategy led to Italy's defeat at the hands of the Habsburg 'ramshackle empire' at Caporetto in 1917. Only considerable assistance from Britain and France and a major national effort made Italy's final victory possible at Vittorio Veneto in 1918. (In order to obtain a united national effort the Italian government had made rash promises, including some regarding future land reform.) Peace proved a major disillusionment, however, and frustrated expectations. The Italian economy experienced difficulty after the currency reconversion, which led to both a rapid increase in inflation and unemployment. The impact of the Bolshevik Revolution on the militant labour movement merely compounded the economic difficulties.

The rise of Fascism

Italian Fascism arose as a result of the collapse of the state after the First World War. Nationally, the short-lived regimes of Vittorio Orlando, Sidney Sonnino, Francesco Nitti, Giolitti, Ivanoe Bonomi and the two governments of Luigi Facta between 1917 and 1922 tried to contain revolutionary activity by turning a blind eye to incidences of social unrest. The political weakness of the state had been made acute by the general-election results of 1919: the liberal centre won only 91 seats, compared with 156 for the socialists and 100 for the Catholic *Populari* (the Italian Popular Party, or *Partito Populare Italiano*, PPI). Political instability increased when the socialists refused to enter into government coalitions, while the so-called 'Roman question' (whereby the Vatican refused to recognise the Italian state) left the Catholic Church in dispute with the Italian state. The combination of frustrated expectations following the First World War and a divided political rulership proved a classic recipe for social crisis.

Political weakness and social appeasement were the consequences of the crisis. The failure of the authorities to intervene against workers' temporary occupation of factories in Milan and Turin in September 1920 or to prevent the agricultural unions from controlling the labour market in the countryside, particularly in the regions of Emilia-Romagna, Tuscany and Apulia, encouraged the disaffected middle class to turn to the *squadristi* (vigilante squads comprising demobilised soldiers) for adequate protection.

Mussolini and the establishment of Fascism

Italian Fascism developed as a fusion of certain left- and right-wing extremist elements. Its dominating force was Benito Mussolini, the former revolutionary socialist who would become *Il Duce*, the leader of Italian Fascism. Although Mussolini was a revolutionary and astute tactician in his early years, his increasing egomania was largely responsible for eventually turning fascism into 'Mussolinism' – a personal dictatorship which played off one faction against another and adroitly compromised with the political establishment.

Before the First World War, Mussolini had been the most revolutionary of Italian socialists, having played a prominent role in the 'red week' uprising in 1914, when he was one of the socialist leaders in a revolutionary attempt to overthrow the state. Like Lenin, Mussolini believed in the potential of a revolutionary war, but, unlike Lenin, he came to regard nationalism rather than proletarian solidarity as a better ideology with which to mobilise the masses. He was sacked as editor of the Socialist Party's newspaper *Avanti* in 1914, and after declaring his enthusiasm for Italy to join the war was expelled from the party. With French financial support he established his own newspaper, *Il Popolo d'Italia*, which advocated intervention. He then fought at the front before being invalided out of the army. Reviled as a traitor by members of the political left after his conversion to Fascism, Mussolini exacted his revenge in the destruction of the workers' political institutions after he came to power.

Mussolini was a marginal figure on the extreme left of Italian politics between 1915 and the general election of 1921. Mussolini established the *Partito Nazionale Fascista* (PNF) in 1919, following the meeting of the 'Fascists of the first hour' at the Piazza San Sepolcro, Milan. In the same year, Fascist candidates stood in Italy's first general election with universal male suffrage. Mussolini received 5,000 out of 270,000 votes in Milan and the Fascists gained only one seat, in Genoa. In 1921, the prime minister, Giolitti, made the mistake of trying to incorporate the Fascists into the nationalist bloc of Giolitti's supporters in the general election; as a result the Fascists obtained 38 seats.

Early Fascist organisational and operational methods

In its early years, before Mussolini became a dictator, the PNF's political structure resembled a form of feudalism. While nominally expressing allegiance to Mussolini, the *ras* (regional Fascist leaders) had full authority in their own localities. They built up their own private armies, the *squadristi*, and generally operated as twentieth-century equivalents of medieval barons, using violence to crush their enemies.

Emulating the theatrical style of politics pioneered during D'Annunzio's occupation of Fiume and the prototypical Fascist rising against Slovene nationalists in the Adriatic port of Trieste in 1919, it was the Fascists of Ferrara and Bologna who were to defeat decisively the threat of revolution in the countryside, using a form of political thuggery that would become one of the most controversial aspects of Fascist methods of operation. Before this development Fascism had been politically irrelevant, but the squads of Italo Balbo (in Ferrara), Dino Grandi (Bologna), Roberto Farinacci (Cremona), Filippo Turati (Brescia) and other intransigent *ras* propelled Fascism into the headlines after November 1920. They were backed by reactionary landlords and capitalist farmers whose aim was to destroy the power of the revolutionary socialists in the countryside. A further element of Fascist support resulted from the rapid growth in the numbers of sharecroppers and peasant leaseholders between 1910 and 1920, particularly in the Po Valley. These agricultural workers were as hostile to the threat of the collectivisation of the land by revolutionary socialists as they were to their landlords and were impressed by misleading Fascist promises regarding the distribution of more land to peasant farmers.

The tacit collusion of the political authorities

Fascism succeeded in becoming a significant force because most of the state authorities tacitly supported political violence against the socialists. Different attitudes to Fascist violence prevailed at the various levels of state power. The prime minister, Giolitti, for example, decreed that incidences of Fascist violence should be opposed by the *Carabinieri* (the police), but his instructions were ignored. When Prefect Cesare Mori, with the backing of the Facta government, tried to stop Fascist syndicates from controlling the movement of workers in Bologna in December 1920, he aroused such hostility that Balbo led squads from all over Emilia-Romagna to Bologna and forced the authorities in Rome to transfer Mori to Apulia. Only at Sarzana, near Genoa, did the authorities try to suppress Fascist violence in July 1921; the resulting reprisals in revenge for the 'fascist martyrs' meant that this response was not repeated.

A marked partiality on the part of the authorities for the Fascists was more typical. At Aguscello, for example, Fascists co-operated in a swoop by the *Carabinieri* in January 1921; after the Fascist squads had violently assaulted trade-union officials, socialists, rather than the Fascist instigators of the violence, were arrested. While Fascist violence was generally ignored in Bologna, the state prosecutors both arrested socialists and treated the boycotts and fines imposed by the unions during agricultural strikes as acts of criminal extortion. Perhaps the most notorious example of the authorities turning a blind eye to Fascist violence occurred in Grossetto, Tuscany, on 30 June 1921, when 55 socialists were murdered by Fascist squads from Florence and Siena; the Fascists went unpunished. Sometimes the police were more directly implicated, as when a bomb planted by a member of the *Carabinieri* near Bergamo, Lombardy, killed two people during a Fascist attack on socialists.

The co-operation between Fascists and the authorities was mirrored by the political manoeuvres of Mussolini. By offering the PNF participation in the nationalist bloc of candidates in the 1921 election, Giolitti gave Mussolini the chance metaphorically to have his cake and eat it too: Fascism was now able to adopt an ambivalent position. While providing squads to terrorise socialist peasants and workers, Fascists could also pose as respectable bourgeois politicians conducting parliamentary deals. Although these contradictory roles inevitably caused internal tensions, Mussolini succeeded in turning the PNF into an effective political party. In the autumn of 1921 Mussolini offered a 'pact of pacification' to the socialists in an attempt to gain respectability and curry influence with the liberals and nationalists. The attempt was immediately disowned by the *ras* and for a time Mussolini was forced to abandon any ideas about turning the PNF into a well-behaved, constitutional party. The intransigent *ras*, however, were eventually forced to recognise that Mussolini's political skills were necessary if the party was to become a significant force on the national stage. On the other hand, the threat of political violence on the part of the Fascists gave them far more political clout than their 38 parliamentary seats warranted.

The 'March on Rome'

Political instability and Mussolini's idea of a potential march on Rome enabled the PNF to continue posing as being constitutionally respectable while still using extremist methods. Its political influence was achieved not through persuasion or

Mussolini and other Fascists march on Rome in October 1922. Why did Fascism appeal to ex-soldiers?

the ballot box but by political thuggery and backstairs political intrigue. The Fascist squads gained local power through political violence aimed at the socialists and the Catholic *Populari* (whose policy of social radicalism was opposed by the Church hierarchy).

In some areas, particularly Emilia-Romagna and Lombardy, Fascism was a mass movement of the radical right, reflecting a genuine middle- and lower-middle-class alliance of peasants, leaseholders, students, bureaucrats, former officers and young people – individuals and groups with little previous political experience who were united by a fear of communism. In other areas, such as Tuscany and Apulia, the rise of Fascism was due more to the intimidating effect of the terrorism and violence meted out by imported Fascist thugs. In much of southern Italy, Fascism was not a significant political factor until after Mussolini had become prime minister in 1922, when membership of the PNF became a prerequisite for political or professional advancement.

The Fascists used the threat of violence to negotiate a deal with the Italian establishment to enable them to make the move from holding local to national power. The so-called 'March on Rome' of 1922, following which Mussolini became prime minister, was only a symbolic coup, however. Mussolini's Fascist squads, as Denis Mack Smith[1] pointed out, 'did not arrive in Rome until twenty-four hours after he had been asked to form a government and only after General Pugliese had orders to let them through'. The myth of the Fascist seizure of power in 1922 was therefore just that – a myth. Mussolini went to Rome by train rather than by marching and owed his appointment to King Victor Emmanuel, who envisaged Mussolini as acting as a bulwark against political and social disorder and a potential communist revolution.

The Fascist state

Mussolini's rise to power did not automatically turn Italy into a Fascist state. The parliamentary weakness of the PNF initially meant that it needed to obtain political allies immediately, as well as to change the political system. The 'March on Rome' led to the formation of a coalition government in which only four members of the first cabinet were Fascists, the majority being nationalists and liberals. While the Italian establishment (the king and his leading political advisers) hoped to tame Mussolini and to neuter Fascist radicalism, Mussolini's aim was to establish a single-party rule and to establish his authority over his followers. By means of political manipulation, Mussolini would eventually achieve both these aims, but the constitutional limitations to his authority and the economic weakness of the Italian state meant that he would never enjoy the same level of authority as that of Hitler in Germany. For Mussolini's retention of power was always dependent on retaining the confidence of Victor Emmanuel. While he generally maintained good personal relations with the king, whose refusal to act over the Fascist 'March on Rome' and the Matteotti crisis (1924) ensured Mussolini's survival, it would be the monarch who would remove Mussolini from power in 1943.

Mussolini's consolidation of power

A position of unchallenged political authority was not fully achieved by Mussolini until 1929. As soon as he became prime minister, Mussolini obtained, by the use of veiled threats, a parliamentary vote in favour of him ruling by decree for a year. By establishing the Fascist Grand Council in 1922, he formed an alternative potential centre of power to the cabinet (although he was careful to make the council a consultative body in order to ensure that it could not challenge his authority). Mussolini also formally incorporated the Fascist squads into the Fascist Voluntary National Militia (MVSM) in 1925 in order to gain greater control over those paramilitary elements who had brought him to power, although he limited their activities to political violence against the left and ceremonial functions rather than allowing them a competing position with the armed services or police. By introducing the Acerbo Law (1923), Mussolini gave the party that won a majority in a general election two-thirds of the total number of parliamentary seats, provided that it obtained 25 per cent of the votes. The gaining of two-thirds of the seats was accordingly achieved by the PNF in the April 1924 election.

In 1923 the Fascists had increased their strength through their amalgamation with the Nationalist Association. This was an important development as it led to a pronounced shift towards the right wing in ideological terms within Italian Fascism, for the elitist, authoritarian and imperialist beliefs of Alfredo Rocco, a leading nationalist theoretician, and Luigi Federzoni, the founder of the Nationalist Association, became important influences on Fascism. The Communist Party was also outlawed after 1922 and the socialists and trade unions emasculated after the 1924 election had reduced them to an insignificant rump.

The Matteotti crisis, 1924

Immediately after the 1924 election, Mussolini faced a major challenge to his authority when the moderate socialist Giacomo Matteotti was murdered by Mussolini's aides. Although not personally implicated in Matteotti's murder, Mussolini's tolerance of political violence made him open to suspicion. Mussolini survived the scandal when, after a period of drifting, it became apparent that there was no effective political alternative to him. The political initiative therefore passed to Mussolini, who moved rapidly to increase his authority, completing his programme of press censorship and the amalgamation of the remaining liberals and members of the *Populari* into the PNF.

After several assassination attempts on Mussolini in 1926, a new, efficient security police, the OVRA (the political police of the Ministry of the Interior), was formed, which accelerated the transition to Mussolini's 'totalitarian' state. It is interesting to note that the OVRA was under the control of the state authorities and its formation did not therefore lead to a 'second wave' of fascism – that is, an outburst of renewed revolutionary activity on the part of the hardcore, intransigent squad of Fascist fanatics.

The Lateran Treaties

In addition to receiving the tacit support of the monarchy, Mussolini also strengthened his political authority through the signing of the Lateran Treaties with Pope Pius XI in 1929, in which Mussolini recognised the Vatican as an independent state under the pope and Catholicism as the state religion. Mussolini had finally healed the rift between the Italian state and the papacy which, despite continued bickering about education between the pope and government during the 1930s, would remain one of Mussolini's enduring achievements.

Fascist disunity

While Mussolini slowly increased his personal power and simultaneously undermined opposition to Fascism, the lack of unity within the Fascist movement increased his indispensability but weakened the coherence of the party. The movement was divided into competing factions, as follows.

1 The 'Fascist left', influenced by Sergio Panunzio, Angelo Olivetti and Edmondo Rossoni, which wished to create a national syndicalist or corporativist state based on Fascist trade unions.
2 The intransigent *ras*, who demanded a 'second wave', a Fascist revolution to replace the institutions of the state with those of the party.
3 Moderate revisionists, like Massimo Rocca, Dino Grandi and Giuseppe Bottai, who argued for a synthesis with the existing political system.

4 Marinetti's Futurists, who demanded the modernisation of the Italian state.
5 Former nationalists, who wanted an aggressive foreign policy.

Mussolini ultimately pursued an essentially opportunistic policy which borrowed from all these components. The problem with the Fascist grand scheme, however, was both that Italians proved to be less than enthusiastic Fascists and that Italy lacked the resources to become a great power.

In 1926 Mussolini made Farinacci, the *ras* of Cremona, party secretary in recognition of the support that the squads had given Mussolini during the Matteotti crisis. But when Farinacci tried to resurrect the demands for a 'second wave' of Fascist revolution Mussolini replaced him with the more pliable Turati in accordance with Mussolini's aim to make the PNF the instrument of state rather than its master. During the 1930s, under Turati's successors Giovanni Giuriati and Achille Starace, membership of the PNF became a matter of expediency rather than a means of gaining entrance to a new political elite.

Mussolini ruled through the institutions of state: maintaining civil order and policing, for example, remained the responsibilities of the traditional authorities under the prefectorial direction of the *Carabinieri* and the security police. The OVRA, the nearest Italian equivalent to the Nazi secret police in Germany, the Gestapo (*Geheime Staatspolizei*), was less effective and under state, not party control, unlike its German counterpart. While there was less political freedom under Fascism than before, the state was not much more oppressive than under the liberal regimes that had preceded it. Fascism used powers of house arrest and exile and persecuted organised-labour groups, but there were few death sentences imposed on its opponents before the 1940s.

The Fascist propaganda machine

Propaganda and persuasion were greater totalitarian influences on the new regime. Mussolini, who was greatly influenced by Gustave Le Bon's theories of crowd psychology and the related practices of contemporary socialist movements, turned the Fascist style into one of political theatre. Through the use of mass rallies, choreographed displays, loudspeakers, new forms of lighting and brass bands, Fascism developed a politics of charisma. The emphasis, particularly under Starace's direction, was on the greatness of the *Duce*, who liked to be filmed driving fast cars and at the controls of tanks or looking down on the diminutive king (official photographs of Mussolini were always taken from below, in order to elongate his small stature).

The 'Fascist style', borrowed from both D'Annunzio's regency in Fiume and Marinetti's histrionic 'happenings', which were organised to advertise Futurism, emphasised mass politics, modernisation, technology, youth and dynamism. The Fascist cult of 'Romanita' suggested that the glories of ancient imperial Rome were about to be reborn in modern Italy. The Fascist 'new man', it was envisaged, would be a living synthesis of the idealised values of the Roman centurion and the supposed dynamism and martial values of the Italian man.

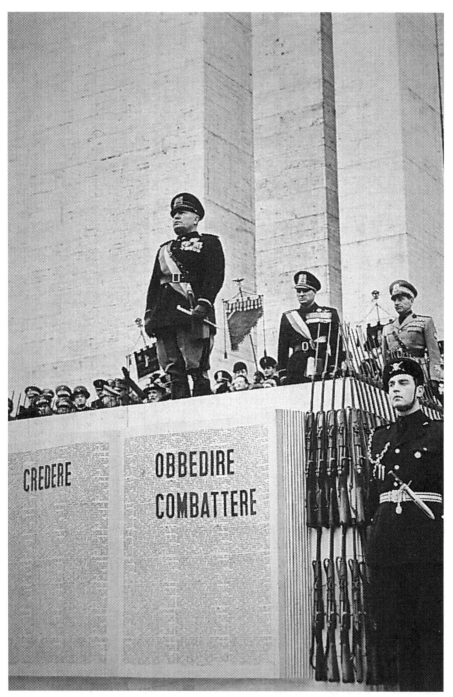

Il Duce, Mussolini, in military uniform, gives a speech from a rostrum containing a typical Fascist slogan: 'Believe', 'obey', 'fight'.

Problems of governance

If the style of charismatic politics emphasised Mussolini's vanity, Fascist propaganda masked the lack of substance that was inherent in most aspects of the regime. Mussolini failed to delegate his authority and was initially responsible for seven ministries; the resulting operational difficulties were further increased by his inability to differentiate between issues of policy formation and routine administration. Mussolini also refused to listen to criticism, so his government rapidly became the preserve of fawning 'yes' men. He was furthermore always careful to change his ministers at regular intervals, in order to prevent a concerted opposition movement emerging.

Mussolini's economic policy

While Mussolini was gradually moving towards the creation of a one-party state and a position of unchallenged personal authority, his inconsistent economic and social policies failed to solve Italy's deep-rooted structural problems. Throughout the inter-war period there was persistent unemployment, which was made worse by the artificial overvaluation of the Italian lire after the currency had been pegged to 'quota 90' (92.45 lire to the £) in 1927 (a more realistic rate would have been 150 lire to the £). This policy, which was instituted for reasons of national prestige, was made worse by the initial adoption of free-trade policies in 1922, which emphasised Italy's economic uncompetitiveness. While the progressive growth of unemployment to a figure of over 1 million after 1928, in addition to the specific chronic underemployment problems of southern Italy, forced the adoption of more protectionist measures after 1927, the severe international depression and threatened collapse of the European banking system (1929–30) led to the failure of the Italian economy to recover. During the 1930s, the move towards a more typically fascist economic policy of autarky was partly a defensive response to conditions in the international economy and partly a political necessity after the League of Nations imposed partial economic sanctions on Italy following the Italian invasion of Abyssinia (Ethiopia) in October 1935.

Many of the new economic policies were misguided, such as the 'Battle for Grain' which, although making Italy self-sufficient in wheat production during the 1930s, led to a misallocation of scarce resources and the considerable weakening of other aspects of the agricultural economy, such as the breeding of livestock. The attempt to increase the national birth rate by means of propaganda exhortation and welfare incentives also failed, despite the dramatic lessening of emigration from Italy during the 1930s, because Italians did not internalise Fascist values. Public-work projects substantially improved the infrastructure of Italy, but Fascist economic policy did not increase productivity. Although there is still considerable debate about economic growth rates under Fascism, a study of the long-term trends does not suggest a pronounced modernisation of the economic base.

The corporate state

The difference between rhetoric and reality was further emphasised by the slow evolution of corporatism under Fascism. Although Fascism claimed to be a 'third way' between capitalism and communism, corporatism proved to be an illusion. The Fascist revolution was supposed to replace parliamentary politics with corporations based on an economic function, with producers', workers' and state interests being equally represented. While steps towards this ideal were first taken with the establishment of syndicates (1925) and some corporations (1934), labour interests were represented only by Fascist unions following the destruction of the labour and socialist movements. State and entrepreneurial interests furthermore proved to be extremely close, even when there were attempts made to differentiate between the two. In practice, having destroyed worker resistance, the Fascists gave manufacturers a free hand with which to manage industry. The Fascist state also encouraged big business through state investment and government contracts.

Similarly, Fascist propaganda was a misleading guide to the social policies of the regime. While Fascist indoctrination became the basis of educational policy, particularly during the 1930s, and, under Starace's influence, membership of the PNF was obligatory for all teachers, whether in primary or higher education, the attempts of Giovanni Gentile (the minister of education from 1922 to 1924) to base educational reform on Fascist nationalistic and idealistic traditions during the 1920s degenerated into Fascist propaganda becoming the basis of the curriculum. Although social control was achieved through the PNF's domination of youth and social organisations, such as the *Opera Nazionale Ballila* (ONB) for boys aged from eight to fourteen years and the national recreational organisation the *Opera Nazionale Dopolavoro* (OND), the evidence suggests that although Italians took full advantage of the increased leisure facilities (hence, perhaps, Italy's impressive performances in soccer's World Cup in 1934 and the Olympic Games in Berlin in 1936), they did not internalise Fascist values.

Mussolini's foreign policy

Fascist foreign policy displayed inconsistencies, for opportunism, rather than ideology, was its primary characteristic between 1922 and 1935. The invasion of Abyssinia in 1935 marked the dividing line between, on the one hand, Mussolini's posturing as the good European statesman and, on the other, the 'Pact of Steel' that he made with Hitler in 1939. Even so, Mussolini's behaviour was never predictable. Mussolini's temporary seizure of Corfu in 1923, after a dispute with Greece, and Italy's economic penetration of Albania in an attempt to increase Italian influence in the Balkans for much of the inter-war period were harbingers of later forms of Fascist imperialism. In contrast, Mussolini's diplomatic efforts in helping to arrange the Munich Conference of 1938 harked back to his earlier willingness to sign pacifying treaties, like the territorial agreement with the Serbo-Croat-Slovene state (1924) and the Locarno Pact (1925), which guaranteed European peace.

Although Mussolini's fate became inextricably linked with that of his fellow dictator, Hitler, Fascist foreign policy was not always in tune with that of Nazism. Fascism was first and foremost an ultra-nationalistic creed and Italian and German interests therefore clashed with regard to the German-speaking minority of the Alto Adige region of northern Italy. Indeed, Mussolini also joined Britain and France in the 'Stresa Front' against German rearmament in 1935. By sending troops to the Brenner Pass, Mussolini furthermore prevented Hitler from marching into Austria in 1934 after the murder of Chancellor Dollfuss. (Hitler was careful to drop his claim to the Alto Adige region after Mussolini had changed sides in 1935, only to incorporate the area into Germany without consulting Mussolini after the latter had been installed as head of the Italian Social Republic in 1943.) Although Hitler admired Mussolini as the first fascist leader, Italy's feeble contribution to the Axis side after its entry into the war on 10 June 1940 meant that the *Duce* was rapidly downgraded by Hitler to a client status. For his part, Mussolini was envious of Hitler's greater success, as well as the resources at his disposal.

By reviving his dreams of imperial Rome with the invasion of Abyssinia, Mussolini showed that his image as a peacemaker was a sham. Sanctions were applied against Italy by the League of Nations, and although these stopped short of an effective oil embargo Mussolini was thrown together with Hitler, who had already taken Germany out of the Disarmament Conference and had left the League of Nations. From then on, Fascism and Nazism were two sides of the same coin, even if Mussolini was increasingly demoted to the position of Hitler's junior partner. In October 1936 the Rome–Berlin Axis (which became the 'Pact of Steel' in May 1939) was formed and Italy later also joined with Germany and Japan in the Anti-Comintern Pact against international communism of November 1936.

The invasion of Abyssinia

The invasion of Abyssinia in October 1935 highlighted the gap between illusion and reality. Italy's 'place in the sun' was a costly enterprise: Abyssinia proved to have few minerals and to possess poor-quality agricultural land. Resources were also squandered by Italy in Libya, where abundant oil reserves remained unexploited. Barbarous methods were used in Abyssinia to defeat poorly armed native tribesmen and chemical warfare and mass-reprisal executions helped the Italian Army to bring the invasion of Abyssinia to a successful conclusion in 1936. Abyssinia and Libya experienced both sides of racist imperialism: they were governed by means of a mixture of paternalism and harsh repression. Fascism in Abyssinia meant the replacement of a medieval form of slavery with a modern version. Countering anti-Italian guerrilla warfare in these countries drained Italian resources until the British destroyed the new Roman empire between 1941 and 1942.

Italian anti-Semitism

It was not until 1938 that anti-Semitism became an official Italian policy. Until then, Italian Fascism had not been anti-Semitic and, indeed, some Jews had been members of the PNF. The introduction of Nuremberg-type race laws and official instructions to the Italian forces to co-operate with the Nazis in the extermination of European Jewry from 1942 showed the extent to which Nazism dominated the Axis by 1941 and how Italian Fascism had become perverted by the 'brutal friendship'. The fact that Italians generally ignored such policies and that the military on occasions sabotaged Nazi plans for the genocide of Jewish people in areas under Italian jurisdiction underlined the collapse of Mussolini's authority over Italy after 1942.

Mussolini's support for foreign forms of fascism

The alliance of, and competition between, Fascist Italy and Nazi Germany was typical of the schizophrenic nature of Mussolini's regime. Mussolini saw himself on occasions as the leader of 'universal fascism', standing at the head of the 'Fascist International' set up at a conference at Montreux in 1934. This proved a stillborn ideal, for fascism was too nationalistic, a fact well understood by Hitler, who only encouraged other forms of fascism when they could be used for 'fifth-column' purposes to aid Nazi objectives. Mussolini was much more indiscriminate in his favours and wasted a considerable amount of foreign-currency exchange by helping to finance foreign forms of fascism, including the British Union of Fascists, in the mistaken belief that they were important influences on both their countries' public opinion and governments.

Mussolini and Hitler also supported the nationalist uprising and Franco's military revolt in Spain in 1936. While the Italian and German provision of munitions and transportation of soldiers from Spanish Morocco to Spain in 1936 was crucial, Italian 'volunteers' were defeated at Guadalajara in 1937, while the sinking of neutral ships by Italian submarines in the Mediterranean worsened international tensions. The difficulties encountered in conquering Albania in 1939 were another sign that Mussolini's appetite was much greater than the ability of Italian resources to maintain the façade of a great-power status. Despite having recently signed the 'Pact of Steel' with Germany, Mussolini was forced to remain a 'non-belligerent' after the outbreak of the Second World War in September 1939, for even he realised that the Italian armed forces were not ready for war and that the navy was no match for British sea power in the Mediterranean. Typically opportunistic, Mussolini entered the war just as France was about to fall in 1940, and even then Italian forces failed to make much of an impression against a demoralised and defeated French army.

The Second World War and the collapse of Fascism

In fact, the Second World War showed Mussolini to be an empty vessel, a boastful buffoon who proved the Achilles heel of the Axis forces. The Italian failure to conquer Greece and the Serbian resistance to the Italian and German invasion of Yugoslavia in 1941 arguably cost Hitler the war because they delayed the German assault on the Soviet Union for six weeks as Hitler was forced to aid his ally. This was a sign of things to come: a catastrophe in Libya was only averted after Hitler had sent the *Afrika Korps*, under Erwin Rommel, to bolster the collapsing Italian forces in February 1941. Even this action only delayed the inevitable: Rommel's defeat at El Alamein in October 1942 led to the Allied landings of Operation Torch in North Africa and the rapid collapse of Axis resistance in this region. From this base, Sicily and then southern Italy were invaded by the Allies in 1943, resulting in the rapid growth of the resistance movement in Italy, with the partisans fighting under communist leadership. Italy was plunged into civil war, a state of affairs which was to last until the final defeat of the Nazis in 1945.

Following the Allied invasion, it would take two years for Fascism finally to collapse in Italy. This had nothing to do with any Italian patriotic support for the Fascist regime but was merely a reflection of the fact that Hitler found it necessary to intervene following Italy's surrender to the Allies in September 1943, when Mussolini was captured and then rescued, in order to shore up his defeated ally once again. Furthermore, the Allies had problems in conquering a difficult geographical terrain which was defended by a professional army of the calibre of the German *Wehrmacht*.

Mussolini, after his dismissal by the king and rescue from imprisonment by the Nazis, was established as a puppet ruler on the banks of Lake Garda. The 'Republic of Salò' (as the Italian Social Republic was sarcastically called because the name reflected Mussolini's greatly reduced status) became notorious for Mussolini's attempted return to his Fascist roots by advocating a syndical form of workers' control of industry and for the brutality of the 'Black Brigades', the security police of the Italian Social Republic which were controlled by the Nazi SS. In fact, both Italians unfortunate enough to live within the republic's jurisdiction and the Nazis ignored the decrees of Mussolini's government. The collapse of Mussolini's authority was symbolised by his death, being shot by Italian partisans near Mezzagra and then being strung up upside down, along with his mistress, from a garage roof in Milan in April 1945.

Contemporary views of Italian Fascism

3.1 The experience of the *ras* of Ferrara

I then announced to the Chief of Police that I would burn down and destroy the houses of all socialists in Ravenna if he did not give me within half an hour the means required for transporting the Fascists elsewhere. It was a dramatic moment. I demanded a whole fleet of trucks. The police officers completely lost their heads, but after half an hour they told me where I could find the trucks already filled with gasoline. Some of them actually belonged to the office of the Chief of Police. My ostensible reason was that I wanted to get the exasperated Fascists out of town; in reality I was organising 'a column of fire' to extend our reprisals throughout the province. We went through all the towns and centres in the provinces of Forli and Ravenna and destroyed and burned all the Red buildings. It was a terrible night. Our passage was marked by huge columns of fire and smoke.

Source: Italo Balbo, *Diario 1922*, Milan, 1932, translated by Charles Delzell, in Charles Delzell (ed.), *Mediterranean Fascism, 1919–45*, London, 1970, p. 37

3.2 The experience of an Italian socialist

At Buscoldo (Mantua) a lorry drew up one night outside the local co-operative club. Darkness had already fallen. With eyes glaring and faces distorted, they shouted: 'Hands up'. The workers present, who were playing cards or reading newspapers, obeyed. The Fascists, revolver in hand, forced them to leave one by one. At the door others were in wait for them with daggers and bludgeons. The workers all had to run the gauntlet. Blows were rained on their heads and shoulders and they were stabbed in the back. Thirty-eight were stabbed, including old men, three disabled soldiers and a fourteen-year-old child. At a blast from a whistle they got back into the lorry, after emptying the till, and disappeared into the night.

Source: A. Rossi,[2] *The rise of Italian Fascism*, London, 1938, p. 109

3.3 Mussolini's view of the Fascist state

But the Fascist State is unique; it is an original creation. It is not reactionary, but revolutionary in that it anticipates the solution of certain universal problems . . . Fascism desires the State to be strong, organic and at the same time founded on a wide popular basis . . . The Fascist State is a will to power and to government. In it the tradition of Rome is an idea that has force. In the doctrine of Fascism Empire is not only a territorial, military or mercantile expression but spiritual or moral . . . Fascism is the doctrine that is most fitted to represent the aims, the states of mind, of a people, like the Italian people, rising again after many centuries of abandonment or slavery to foreigners.

Source: Benito Mussolini, 'The political and social doctrine of Fascism',[3] in A. Lyttleton (ed.), *Italian Fascism from Pareto to Gentile*, London, 1973, pp. 55–57

3.4 The peasants' view of the PNF

The gentry were all Party members, even the few like Dr. Millillo who were dissenters. The Party stood for Power, as vested in the Government and State, and they felt entitled to a share of it. For exactly the opposite reason none of the peasants were members; indeed it was unlikely that they should belong to any political party whatever, should, by chance, another exist. They were not Fascists, just as they would never have been Conservatives or Socialists or anything else. Such matters had nothing to do with them; they belonged to another world and they saw no sense in them. What had the peasants to do with Power, Government and the State? The state, whatever form it might take, meant the 'fellows in Rome'. 'Everyone knows', they said, 'that the fellows in Rome don't want us to live like human beings. There are hailstorms, landslides, droughts, malaria and . . . the State. These are inescapable evils.'

Source: Carlo Levi,[4] *Christ stopped at Eboli*, London, 1982, pp. 77–78, quoted in J. Whittam, *Fascist Italy*, Manchester, 1995, p. 154

1 What do the sources suggest about the nature of Italian Fascism?

2 What do the sources suggest about the reactions of Italians to Fascism?

3 What do the sources tell us about Italian Fascist political violence?

4 What do the sources suggest about the failure of Mussolini to create a 'new Fascist man'?

Notes and references

1 Denis Mack Smith, *Mussolini*, London, 1981, p. 40.

2 'A. Rossi' was the pseudonym of the Italian socialist Angelo Tasca. The book was published when he was in exile in Paris and was later translated into English.

3 This text is taken from the second half of the article 'Fascism', written for the *Enciclopedia Italiana* by Giovanni Gentile and Benito Mussolini in 1932.

4 Levi was exiled from 1933 to 1935 for anti-Fascist activities. This account, written in 1944, was first published in the following year.

4 Hitler and Nazism

Nazism was the most radical form of fascism and by far the most important. Although it was a dynamic form of fascism, Nazism was different in many ways from the Italian prototype. Unlike Italian Fascism, the core Nazi beliefs combined racism with a strange conspiracy theory: the alleged plot of Jewish bankers and communists internationally to destroy the world's nation states and replace them with a universal government.

In practice, the Nazi revolution turned out to be a 'revolution of destruction', not only in the sense of the Second World War which Hitler provoked, reducing much of Germany and Europe to rubble, but also in the way in which Germany's social structure was undermined by the Nazis between 1933 and 1945. Hitler both defeated the attempts of the German conservative establishment to restrain him by implementing the process of 'co-ordination' (*Gleichschaltung*) between 1933 and 1934 and imposed Nazi values on everyday German life. This occurred to a greater extent than Fascist ideas were imposed on Italy and the process was accelerated after 1939. Although it was a complex procedure, Hitler proved himself to be both a skilled political manipulator and tactician and an original (if ultimately flawed) military strategist. But he was also, above all, a rabid ideologist. As a result of his actions, the Hitler state destroyed the legacy of imperial and Weimar Germany and undermined the humane values of German culture, which led to the catastrophe of 1945 with the defeat and political and geographical division of the country.

The rise of Nazism

Unlike in Italy, the rise of fascism in Germany occurred in one of the world's most advanced economies, for the German modernisation and industrialisation processes during the nineteenth century had helped to create a powerful state. It needed an unparalleled series of catastrophes in the early twentieth century to undermine the German humanistic culture and to reverse the slowly developing liberal and democratic influences that existed in an authoritarian society. Political extremism in Germany developed from the failure of state and society to manage the complex problems arising from the country's sudden defeat at the end of the First World War in 1918. As a result of this deep trauma, the most virulent, radical and amoral version of fascism was to develop.

Although the First World War created the necessary conditions to enable the rise of Nazism, Nazi ideology was derived from the intellectual and political underworld of pre-1914 Germany. Before 1914, this far-right ideology, which was heavily focused on anti-Semitism, remained on the political fringe and had little influence on domestic politics. Hitler himself, for example, although later greatly influenced by the Austrian anti-Semitism of Karl Lueger (1844–1910) and Georg von Schönerer (1842–1921), was a failed art student and architect whose personal idleness prevented him enjoying the bourgeois lifestyle that he craved. He, like other social failures in the German and Austro-Hungarian empires, found in anti-Semitism – 'the socialism of fools', as the German social democratic leader August Bebel (1840–1913) called it – a convenient explanation for their own shortcomings, although there is little evidence that Hitler became an anti-Semite before 1914, despite his claims to the contrary.

The legacy of the First World War

The circumstances surrounding the downfall of imperial Germany in 1918 fatally weakened the infant Weimar Republic that followed it. The German military, led by Paul von Hindenburg and Erich Ludendorff, refused to accept responsibility for Germany's defeat and created the myth (the *Dolchstoßlegende*) that the soldiers fighting for their country had been 'stabbed in the back' by Jews and Bolsheviks while they were at war. The sole responsibility for signing the Versailles Treaty was left to the leaders of the new Weimar Republic, who were consequently attacked by right-wing nationalists for 'betraying' Germany. In reality, as von Hindenburg and Ludendorff well knew, Germany had suffered a total military defeat in November 1918 and the Weimar politicians had therefore had no option but to sign the punitive Versailles Treaty in 1919: a refusal to do so would have meant that the Allied powers would have restarted the war. Nevertheless, throughout the inter-war period up to 1933 it was the Weimar democracy which bore the odium for signing what many Germans regarded as the Versailles '*Diktat*' (dictate), although it had only come into being on 9 November 1918. The harsh terms were blamed on the politicians who had tried to cope with the war's consequences, not on the wartime leaders who were ultimately responsible for Germany's plight.

The rise of Nazism resulted from the failure of the victors to establish a viable and stable new Europe. By the terms of the Versailles Treaty, the creation of the so-called 'Polish Corridor' (which gave Poland access to the sea) meant that much German territory was lost in the east, while Alsace-Lorraine was returned to France (having been ceded to the newly independent Germany in 1871 after the Franco-Prussian War). The size of the *Reichswehr* (German army) was limited to 100,000 men and the Rhineland was made a demilitarised zone in which the Germans could station no troops while the Allies could keep soldiers there for a period of 15 years. Worst of all, from the German point of view, were the reparations clauses, which made Germany responsible for all the damage done by its forces in occupied France and Belgium, as well as the notorious 'war-guilt' clause (Article 231), which forced Germany to admit responsibility for starting the First World War. These clauses were bitterly resented by the German people.

The fact that the Weimar government was forced to sign this 'slave treaty', as some Germans called it, fatally weakened its authority from the outset. It came under immediate attack from members of the far left, extremists who wanted a socialist workers' state, and also from extreme right-wingers, who hated the Weimar democracy and wanted a return to some form of authoritarian rule.

The challenge to the Weimar Republic

The initial challenge to the Weimar Republic came from the left in January 1919, with the Spartacist uprising in Berlin, a revolutionary revolt by left-wing independent socialists, militant shop stewards and communists trying to emulate the Bolshevik Revolution and establish a Soviet government in Germany, led by the Marxists Rosa Luxemburg and Karl Liebknecht. The uprising was crushed by the *Freikorps* ('free corps'), a right-wing militia to which, following the collapse of the military, the majority-socialist government was forced to turn to help to restore order. Then followed the *Freikorps'* destruction of Kurt Eisner's Soviet-style regime (which had been set up in Bavaria in November 1918) in April 1919. (It is interesting to note that Hitler was in Munich, the capital of Bavaria, at this time.)

The republic, whose survival depended on a deal which its president, Friedrich Ebert, had been forced to make with the *Reichswehr* because of the lack of reliable state military and revolutionary police units and the need ruthlessly to crush the revolutionary left, was then attacked by right-wing opponents in March 1920. An attempted *Putsch* (*coup d'état*) was staged in Berlin by Wolfgang Kapp, but he and his *Freikorps* supporters were defeated by a combination of a lack of army support and a general strike by workers.

Another challenge to the authority of the Weimar Republic came from the infant National Socialist German Workers' Party (*Nationalsozialistische Deutsche Arbeiterpartei*, NSDAP, or Nazi Party) in Munich in November 1923, whose so-called 'Beerhall *Putsch*' followed the French invasion of the Ruhr region of Germany in January 1923 in reprisal for Germany having defaulted on its reparations payments. The French occupation was bitterly resented and the Nazi leader, Adolf Hitler, along with his collaborator, Ludendorff, determined to overthrow the Bavarian government in a prelude to a 'march on Berlin'. In the event, however, he could not raise enough military or popular support to do so and Hitler and his followers were routed in the centre of Munich when the police fired on them. Hitler was given only a light, five-year jail sentence, however, which reflected the right-wing bias of the German judiciary (in the event Hitler served only nine months in Landsberg prison). He used the time to dictate his book, *Mein Kampf* ('My struggle'), and to absorb an important lesson: never again would the Nazi movement attempt to overthrow the Weimar Republic by force, although its hatred of the republic remained undiminished.

Economic instability

Given the turbulent circumstances, the Weimar Republic did well to survive the period from 1919 to 1923. Even more so since the French occupation of the Ruhr,

Germany's largest industrial area, provoked a policy of passive resistance on the part of German workers in 1923, which contributed to massive hyper inflation in that year. The value of the German currency, the mark, collapsed in a spectacular fashion and was only restored as a result of the massive programme of American loans that was set up by the 1924 Dawes Plan. Even during the period between 1924 and 1929, which was one of relative stability, the Weimar economy became unhealthily dependent on such short-term loans.

The fact that the economic blockade of central Europe by the Allied powers was not lifted until after the peace treaties had been signed between 1919 and 1920 created conditions which encouraged the advance of the Bolshevik Revolution into central and eastern Europe. The Weimar Republic had been seriously threatened by the Spartacist revolt (1919), the Bavarian revolution (1918–19), the attempted militaristic coup of the Kapp *Putsch* (1920) and the 'Beerhall *Putsch*' (1923). It was also weakened by the massive monetary expansion after the war, when it printed money to fund reparations, social welfare and the transition to the peacetime economy, which accelerated into hyper-inflation from 1922 to 1923 and decimated the value of middle-class savings, as well as by the French occupation of the Rhineland from 1923 to 1924. Even during the period of stability of the so-called 'Stresemann years' (1924–29) – when Gustav Stresemann was Germany's foreign minister – following the establishment of the Rentenmark (valued at 1 billion old marks), which stabilised the currency, and the return of American investment, German agriculture failed to benefit from the upturn in economic growth. The reasons for the failure of the Weimar Republic have led to sharp debate, but the banking collapse of 1930 and the subsequent withdrawal of American investment meant that the generous welfare expenditure of Weimar Germany could not be sustained.

It was the impact of the Great Depression (1929–33) which encouraged the electorate to vote for extremist parties like the NSDAP and the Communist Party (*Kommunistische Partei Deutschlands*, KPD) and which precipitated the withdrawal of US short-term loans which the Weimar Republic could not redeem. The Nazi Party's electoral breakthrough came in 1930, when its vote rose to 5 million and it won 107 seats in the Reichstag (the German parliament), a leap from 2.6 per cent to 18.3 per cent of the vote. This figure rose to 37.3 per cent in the July 1932 election, although it slipped slightly to 33.1 per cent in November 1932.

From 1930 the Weimar Republic became subject to authoritarian rulership. Under successive chancellors (Heinrich Brüning, 1930–32; Franz von Papen, 1932; and Kurt von Schleicher, 1932–33) the constitution was abrogated by President von Hindenburg, the former field marshal and erstwhile supporter of the *Kaiser* (emperor) who had become the republic's president in 1925, through the use of Article 48. Article 48, which was supposed to be invoked only in times of emergency, allowed the government to rule without reference to the Reichstag. Between 1930 and 1933, however, von Hindenburg, who enjoyed tremendous prestige among the populace as a former war hero, used it to rule permanently through chancellors who were all his personal favourites. A study by Henry Ashby Turner[1] has also emphasised the influence of members of the presidential clique, like Otto Meissner, von Hindenburg's chief of staff, and von Hindenburg's son, Oskar, on the president during this period.

The 'alternative revolution'

Hitler's rise to power is a complex story, but the main factors in his political elevation were the succession of crises following the First World War and the failure of the Weimar system to cope with the consequences of Germany's defeat in 1918, the frustrated expectations arising from the apparent recovery of stability during the 'Stresemann years', followed by a return to an economically catastrophic situation between 1929 and 1932, when the government failed to reverse the inexorable rise in the unemployment statistics. Both Weimar democracy and authoritarian government failed to institute a recovery, and for most Germans the alternative, in the form of the potential threat to their private property, violence and terror of a communist revolution, was unthinkable. As a result, the 'alternative revolution' of the Nazis was believed to be the only viable option by many Germans.

In fact, Hitler was fortunate in that by the time he came to power in 1933 the Young Plan, which revised the Dawes Plan, had scaled down the level of German reparations in 1929; Brüning had negotiated a moratorium in 1932 and had instituted deflationary policies designed to tackle the massive budget deficit and to cut state welfare and unemployment benefits (Brüning was then swept off course by a further banking collapse, however). The imaginative unbalanced budgets and public-works programmes put in place by the von Papen and von Schleicher administrations would furthermore benefit Hitler's regime once their fiscally stimulating effects had enabled the economy to begin to recover.

Hitler's leadership strategy

After Hitler's economic good fortune has been acknowledged, the question remains as to why the Nazis were the beneficiaries of the German catastrophe after 1929. A key factor in their success was the constant underestimation of Hitler's potential significance by such figures as chancellors Brüning, von Papen and von Schleicher. Hitler consistently refused to accept anything less than the post of chancellor from 1932 to 1933 and held his party together when its vote began to fall in the November 1932 Reichstag elections. Von Hindenburg's refusal to make Hitler (by then the leader of the largest party in the Reichstag) chancellor allowed Hitler justly to claim that the government was being undemocratic.

From the moment that Hitler became a political animal, when he joined Anton Drexler's German Workers' Party (*Deutsche Arbeiterpartei*, DAP) in 1919, a year before it became the National Socialist German Workers' Party, he rapidly developed his unique political style. Although his bohemian working habits gave him an air of indolence and he demonstrated a marked deficiency in administrative and bureaucratic skills, his fanaticism, ruthlessness and charisma, allied to his belief in his personal destiny, his inflexible political strategy and his tactical cunning, combined to produce a formidable politician (even if his overwhelming

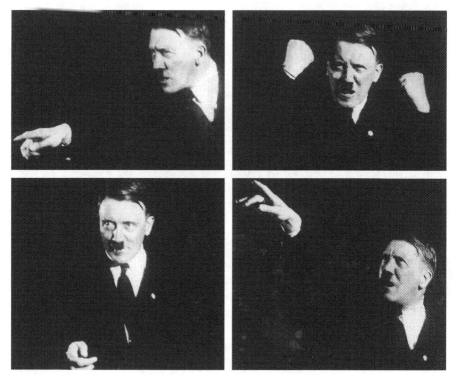

Heinrich Hoffman's photographs show Hitler practising oratorical gestures. Like Mussolini, Hitler was aware how speeches were a powerful propaganda device for influencing mass audiences. What other propaganda methods did fascists use?

arrogance would lead to his ultimate downfall). Unlike Mussolini, Hitler devolved routine administration and party matters to his acolytes while at the same time keeping them fanatically loyal, binding them to him personally through both the oath of allegiance that they were required to swear to him and the *Führerprinzip* (the 'principle of leader', by which Hitler was acknowledged as the sole source of political authority).

Hitler's achievement during the period before he came to power was to unite all the *völkisch* (nationalistic), racist fringe parties under his leadership and to undermine the nationalistic right. His personal hold over his followers created the impression of a united party devoted to its *Führer* ('leader'), a characteristic which would be transmitted to the masses during the Great Depression and which proved particularly potent in Protestant rural areas and amongst the middle classes. Hitler's charisma and the dynamism of the Nazis convinced many that only the NSDAP had the answer to the agricultural depression and a non-communist solution for unemployment which would safeguard private property. Hitler transformed the NSDAP from a party which was ready to use violence to achieve power (a strategy which had been a spectacular failure in 1923) into one which was committed to its achievement by peaceful means. The failed 'Beerhall *Putsch*' also turned Hitler – 'the drummer', or foot soldier, of the German nationalistic movement, who had thereby learned his lesson – into the 'man of destiny' who had an unshakable belief in his own political will.

In fact, Hitler was very much concerned with disguising his tactics with a veneer of legality, for German Nazism was responsible for even greater political violence than Italian Fascism. In 1932, for example, 14,005 claims were made on the compulsory insurance scheme of the *Sturmabteilung* (the SA, the paramilitary arm of the NSDAP), and in the first half of that year 70 Nazis were killed as a result of street violence.

The last days of the Weimar Republic

The rapid rise of Nazism was not irresistible, however. The division between the social democrats, who had created the Weimar Republic, and the communists on the left, who sought to overthrow it, certainly assisted Hitler (this division went back to 1919), but his refusal to accept anything less than the chancellor-ship, together with the fall in the proportion of the Nazi vote late in 1932, made him vulnerable. This was what made the ineptitude of other politicians so significant.

Although Brüning's deflationary strategy of 1930 of cutting government expenditure increased Germany's economic misery in the short term, it did lead to the return of international confidence for a time and allowed for a moratorium on reparations to be negotiated. However, the Protestant von Hindenburg's distrust of his Catholic chancellor led to Brüning's dismissal in May 1932 and his replacement by the diplomat and von Hindenburg's fellow East Prussian *Junker* (aristocratic landowner) von Papen. Von Papen had the full confidence of von Hindenburg, but his potential electoral support provided far too narrow a base for him to form a successful government and he was manipulated out of power by the intrigues of his successor, von Schleicher, in December 1932. Von Papen then plotted in turn to remove von Schleicher, helped by the latter's inability to divide the NSDAP, to gain the confidence of the trade unions or to form a viable coalition government. It was in these circumstances that Hitler agreed to accept the chancellorship in January 1933. For his part, Hitler thought that it was now prudent to assume the position, given the decline in the Nazi vote between the July and November 1932 elections which indicated that support for the Nazis had peaked.

Hitler's rise to power owed much to the mistakes of others and especially to the folly of von Papen, who persuaded the president to make Hitler chancellor on 30 January 1933, although von Hindenburg could not abide Hitler personally and contemptuously referred to him as the 'Bohemian corporal' (Hitler had indeed been a corporal during the First World War, but was an Austrian, rather than a Bohemian, by birth). Von Papen, who announced to the world that 'we've hired Hitler', believed that Hitler would be a pliable stooge in a cabinet in which he, von Papen, would be vice chancellor and would therefore be in a position to protect the establishment's interests and the social power of the *Junker* landed elite.

The process of *Gleichschaltung*

The conviction of Marinus van der Lubbe, a Dutch communist, for burning down the Reichstag in Berlin in February 1933 led to the banning of the KPD, and the Nazi propaganda machine was at full blast in the March 1933 general election. Despite their exploitation of the communist 'threat', the NSDAP won only 43.9 per cent of the popular vote in the last free elections that would be held in Germany for over a decade. Hitler, however, was able to secure the passage of his Enabling Act with the support of all the other parties in the Reichstag apart from the social democrats, who voted against it. The Enabling Act authorised Hitler to dispense with the Reichstag and rule by decree. German democracy was dead.

There followed a process of *Gleichschaltung* ('co-ordination', or 'bringing into line'), during which every area of German life was Nazified. It was a process by which Nazi values infiltrated society through co-ordinating state and party functions. Overlapping jurisdiction, the establishment of parallel party and state agencies and the lack of a clear division of power between competing institutions led to a creeping Nazification of the state, as ambitious Nazis carved out empires of influence for themselves. Free trade unions were abolished and replaced by a Nazi labour front. All other political parties were banned, although the large Catholic *Zentrumspartei* (Centre Party) agreed to dissolve itself in exchange for an

Compulsory Spontaneous Demonstration (David Low, 1 May 1934). What feature of fascism is satirised in this cartoon which appeared in the London *Evening Standard*?

agreement between Hitler and Pope Pius XI which would safeguard the position of the Church in Germany. Nazi racial doctrine was enshrined in the new Civil Service Law, which expelled Jewish civil servants from their posts. It remained only for Hitler's able henchman, Joseph Goebbels, to take control of the German media and thereby prevent freedom of expression in Germany.

The 'Night of the Long Knives'

Yet Hitler's power, like Mussolini's, was temporarily subject to constitutional restraint. Until the death of von Hindenburg, in August 1934, he could still have been dismissed by the president if Hitler lost von Hindenburg's confidence. Hitler was also aware that the SA, which had been very useful in destroying the labour movement, was now a diminishing asset, being negatively perceived by both the public and the *Reichswehr*. Hitler therefore decided to neutralise the threat to social stability posed by the SA. On 30 June 1934, the 'Night of the Long Knives', Hitler settled the score with the SA leader Ernst Röhm, who had been demanding a merger between his enormous paramilitary force and the regular army. Röhm's peremptory execution, together with those of other leading SA men, removed the threat of a 'second revolution' which would have broken the power of those very industrial and landowning elites whose support Hitler needed in order to stay in power and also secured the loyalty of the *Reichswehr*. At the same time, Hitler also took the opportunity to have murdered the former chancellor, von Schleicher, as well as Gregor Strasser, a former leader of the radical, anti-capitalist wing of the party.

Despite its illegal nature and ruthlessness, Hitler's action proved a popular move. It was a signal to the establishment that, although they were prepared to employ state terror and commit political murder, the Nazis were committed to working through the main institutions of state, that the SA would be subordinated to the *Reichswehr* and that Hitler, it believed, was no threat to conservative interests. What was not realised was that those most implicated in the events of 30 June 1934, Heinrich Himmler's SS (*Schutzstaffel*, 'protective echelon'), would prove a much more sinister threat to traditional values in the long term than the SA had ever been.

By removing political opposition to the NSDAP, destroying a potential power base in the form of the SA and by assuming the powers of the presidency himself on the death of von Hindenburg, Hitler was now in a position to exert his authority, untrammelled by any hindrances.

The Hitler state

Following the death of von Hindenburg, after August 1934 Hitler's power was not constrained by any constitutional limits. By combining the posts of president and chancellor, Hitler succeeded in removing both any potential legal challenge to his position and the ability of any authority to dismiss the *Führer*. (In practice, however, Hitler still thought it necessary not to alienate important vested interests within the state, such as the *Junkers*, big business, the *Reichswehr* and civil servants, until at least 1938, when he took personal control of the *Reichswehr*.) The chief limitations on Hitler's authority therefore arose from his own personal habits and not from any institutional or constitutional controls.

The intentionalist–structuralist debate

Much of the analysis of the nature of the Nazi state has become focused around the intentionalist–structuralist debate. One group of historians, the intentionalists, represented by individuals like Alan Bullock and K. D. Bracher, sees Hitler's intention as explaining everything that happened in the Third Reich (the Third German Empire which Hitler had proclaimed as being the successor to the Holy Roman Empire and that of 1871–1918). By contrast, the structuralists see the structure of the Third Reich, a chaotic, badly run regime that was weakened by Hitler's sloppy governmental methods, as being instrumental. According to one structuralist, Hans Mommsen,[2] Hitler was, in fact, 'a weak dictator' and under him Germany was 'polycratic' – that is, it had many rival power bases centred around leading Nazis like Goebbels, Himmler and Hermann Göring.

It is possible, however, to see Hitler as a lazy and inefficient dictator but also one who, as his deputy from 1938, Göring, said, was the ultimate source of authority in Germany. 'Weakness' in this sense does not mean that Hitler ever lacked personal ruthlessness, as his elimination of the SA leaders and other politicians during the 'Night of the Long Knives' and his authorisation of the mass murder of the Jews during the Second World War show. It merely recognises Hitler's boredom with bureaucracy and everyday government: 'A moment of genius', he once said, 'is worth a lifetime of office work'.

This contradiction in the view of Hitler's authority had its origin in the *Führer*'s personality. Hitler was obsessed with not compromising his personal authority, with maintaining his personal prestige at all costs, and refused to take sides in disputes until a clear winner had emerged or to take decisions unless they were absolutely forced on him, while he intervened only rarely in aspects of domestic politics except when it was absolutely necessary to do so in order to preserve his authority. Such erratic behaviour often disguised Hitler's real influence on events.

The image of the Nazi government was that presented by Goebbels' Propaganda Ministry, of the 'well-oiled Nazi machine', creating an efficient, united, harmonious and totalitarian state. The reality was a disorganised, dynamic squabble of competing interests fighting for influence in a ruthless, social Darwinian battle in which victory went to the strongest. There were few rules in the Nazi political game, except that the personal authority of the *Führer* should never be questioned. For Hitler, personal loyalty to him was the linchpin of the whole system. Indeed, the nearest analogy to Nazi government is that offered by feudalism, so that the authority of the *Führer* was cemented by the individual oath of loyalty made to Hitler. Even the *Reichswehr* voluntarily introduced a personal oath of loyalty to Hitler in August 1934, which destroyed its independence and subordinated its officer corps to Hitler's will. (The oath provided members of the German army with an excuse for their effective collusion in the mass murder, genocide and barbaric behaviour on the Eastern

Front, in a post-war attempt to avoid responsibility and become compromised by the worst criminal activities of the Second World War.)

Hitler and the NSDAP

The process of *Gleichschaltung*, the co-ordination of state and party in the Nazi system, was resolved by duplicating areas of authority and making the demarcation of the responsibilities of competing institutions vague. Hitler's dilemma lay in not alienating establishment interests while at the same time maintaining the enthusiasm of the NSDAP and the SA. It was also necessary to retain the specialist expertise of civil servants rather than replacing them with either NSDAP members with revolutionary ideas or the 'old fighters'. When fresh impetus or policies were needed, Hitler often set up new agencies or administrative units which were accountable to him alone and which often competed for influence with existing institutions.

Thus the Four-year Plan Department (intended to make Germany economically self-sufficient), which operated under Göring after 1936, usurped many of the functions of the Ministry of Economics by issuing a number of rearmament contracts. After the defeat of Göring's *Luftwaffe* (military air-force) in the Battle of Britain in 1940, and in response to the urgent need to increase Germany's productivity and to establish a more rigorous war economy in 1942, Hitler established the *Organization Todt* under Fritz Todt (after Todt's death, in February 1942, he appointed Albert Speer his successor and minister of armaments and production) to cut through the bureaucratic red tape and develop new weapons and establish underground factories in order to enable Germany to prolong the war. Remarkably, given the effects of the massive Allied bombing raids on Germany and the German army's continuing defeat on the Eastern Front, Germany's collapse was averted by such methods. Similarly, the growth of the SS was encouraged to provide an alternative intelligence organisation, while the placing of the secret-police force, the Gestapo (*Geheime Staatspolizei*), under the control of Himmler, the chief of the SS, in 1934 enabled the Nazis to gain complete authority over the police.

Indeed, the method by which legal processes were subverted and brought under Nazi control provides a textbook demonstration of how a state can be brought under totalitarian domination by means of co-ordination, infiltration and the establishment of parallel agencies. The initial use of the SA as 'auxiliaries' to the police in Prussia between 1932 and 1933, the rapid expansion of the Gestapo in size and influence and the establishment of concentration camps from 1933 was paralleled by the willingness of the legal authorities to compromise their judicial independence by failing to question the dubious new criteria for the basis of Nazi legislation, as well as the blatant undermining of civil liberties and the rule of law by the actions of the Nazi state. This legal collusion was epitomised by the authorities' failure to investigate the atrocities committed during both the 'Night of the Long Knives' and *Kristallnacht* ('crystal night', named after the shards of broken glass from the smashed windows of Jewish-owned properties), the SA pogrom against the Jews, in 1938.

It would be a mistake to see all Nazi actions as those intended to subvert the agencies of state, however, for on occasions Hitler deliberately marginalised NSDAP bodies. Hitler's destruction of the SA's leadership in 1934 was partly intended as a signal that the *Reichswehr* would not be subordinated to, or supplanted by, the NSDAP's militia, although the *Reichswehr* became increasingly subjected to the *Führer*'s personal control. Similarly, *Gleichschaltung* did not necessarily entail the centralisation of government under Nazi control. The attempt to centralise government by Hans Lammers, head of the Reich Chancellery, and Wilhelm Frick, the minister of the interior, was partially successful, in that it brought the regional civil service under Nazi influence, but it foundered because of the direct link to Hitler that was enjoyed by the *Gauleiter* (Nazi regional administrative leaders). It was not until after the war was clearly lost that Martin Bormann, the head of the Nazi chancellery after 1941, was able to outmanoeuvre his rivals and use his position as Hitler's personal secretary to control access to the *Führer*.

The complexity of the Nazi operational system should not detract from the fact that Hitler was the fulcrum around which all else revolved. The bureau-cratic proliferation of overlapping state and party institutions enabled Hitler to evade political decision-making except when his intervention was crucial to maintain his prestige and authority. The Nazi system was based on ideological principles: by providing few guidelines, the social Darwinian survival of the fittest or most ruthless ensured the radicalisation of government. It also allowed, and encouraged, Nazi infiltration of, or pressure on, state institu-tions, thus encouraging a constant, if gradual, increase of the Nazification of the decision-making process. Although the system encouraged potential conflict, Hitler was not worried by the power accumulated by other Nazi leaders. Thus Hitler seemed quite at ease with Göring's massive accumulation of power and influence during the 1930s and also with Himmler's during the war. The importance of the oath of personal loyalty to Hitler and the *Führer-prinzip* that prevailed at all levels of the party and state meant there were few institutional controls and little scope for effective criticism of Hitler within the Third Reich.

The survival of the Nazi state during the 1930s was a consequence of many factors, including the recovery of the German economy, foreign-policy successes, Goebbels' mastery of propaganda and the establishment of a repressive state apparatus which monitored and controlled all expressions of dissent and resistance. In fact, the last factor was relatively less important than the preceding three, for what is particularly interesting was the degree of public consent and approval manifested for the regime, especially for the role of the *Führer*, as seen not only in the reports on public opinion compiled by the Propaganda Ministry but also in the secret reports made by the Sopade, the social democrats' intelligence organisation. While the NSDAP acted as the focus for the people's grumbles about the regime, the development of the 'Hitler myth' ensured that Hitler remained a powerful integrating figure.

Nazi economic policy

The success of the 'Nazi economic recovery', as claimed by the Nazis, provided the basis for the development and survival of the regime. From a figure of 33 per cent unemployed in January 1933 a slow, but persistent, economic recovery, which accelerated after 1935, enabled full employment levels to be reached by 1938, while there were significant inflationary pressures evident by the time of the outbreak of war in 1939. Nazi economics reflected the primacy of politics: there was no coherent economic programme put in place, merely the taking of an ad hoc series of emergency initiatives designed to insulate the German economy from the influence of the international economy, combined with the gradual creation of an autarkic, or self-sufficient, position based on the stockpiling of raw materials. Nazi economic policies were not based on the market allocation of scarce resources but on the political imperatives of reducing unemployment while maintaining standards of living and, after 1935, of instituting a massive rearmament programme. In fact, Göring's rhetorical question 'Guns or butter?' became, until the setbacks of the war induced a mood of greater realism, a policy of guns *and* butter. The plunder and booty taken during the rapid *Blitzkrieg* ('lightning war') conquests of much of Europe between 1939 and 1941 enabled Hitler to augment his domestic economic success, at least in the short term. War, however, was a political, not an economic, decision.

Although the principle of private property was respected by the Nazis, the rapid expansion of government expenditure after 1935 meant that greater management of the economy was exerted as a consistently higher proportion of gross domestic product (GDP) became dependent on state employment. The awarding of state contracts, with the highest priority being given to rearmament, led to a form of state capitalism in which the government increasingly allocated resources and dominated the market, particularly after Göring's Four-year Plan Department usurped many of the functions of the Ministry of Economics.

The principles by which Nazi economic policies were implemented were surprisingly conservative. Under the policies of the conservative banker Hjalmar Schacht (the minister of economics from 1934 to 1939), rigorous foreign-exchange controls restricted imports and exports to the essentials, based on the principle of bilateral trade and the economics of barter. By such draconian methods, balance-of-payments problems were kept under control and policies of import substitution and manufacturing synthetic alternatives were introduced. This last policy accounts for the key role of the chemical industry, particularly the firm of I. G. Farben, in the Third Reich.

While public expenditure and the public-works projects of Hitler's immediate predecessors were rapidly expanded, the means of paying for them was quite orthodox. Inflationary pressures were initially not a problem, given the unused resources within the economy, but as recovery progressed the Nazis' insistence on price and dividend controls and forced investment kept the potential problem under check. The provision of so-called '*mefo*' bills, a form of unofficial accounting, also disguised the amount of money being spent on rearmament.

Despite his expenditure on rearmament, one of Hitler's top priorities was to ensure that living standards did not fall to unacceptable levels. Token schemes, like the production of the Volkswagen, the 'people's car' (although no German worker actually had one), were designed to win over public opinion. So, too, were the cruises to Norway and the Canary Islands arranged by the *Kraft durch Freude* ('Strength through Joy') organisation.

Hitler's foreign policy

Hitler's economic policy was closely linked to his foreign-policy goals, which were as follows.

1 To overturn the Versailles Treaty and restore Germany to its former position as a great power.
2 To create a *Großdeutschland* ('Greater Germany') by bringing ethnic Germans living in Austria, the Czechoslovakian Sudetenland and, ultimately, the 'Polish Corridor' into the Reich.
3 To obtain *Lebensraum* ('living space') in the east for the German people (the USSR was the special focus of this policy). Because, in Hitler's racist view, these areas were inhabited by 'sub-human' Slavs, he rationalised that it was legitimate for the 'racially superior' Germans to annexe the Slavs' territory.

Hitler's foreign-policy achievements during the 1930s, which were approved of by German public opinion, included the remilitarisation of the Rhineland (1936), the *Anschluss* (union) with Austria (1938) and the annexation of the Sudetenland (1938) and rump of Czechoslovakia (1939).

In order to achieve all his foreign-policy objectives, Hitler needed a dynamic economy allied to a massive rearmament programme. When it broke out in 1939, war was unwelcome, because Hitler calculated that the invasion of Poland would not lead to war. For Hitler, it came three to four years too early because the Four-year Plan had not yet produced the level of armaments required to win the war easily. It also involved Germany in a conflict in the west, something which Hitler had wanted to avoid but brought upon himself by his flagrant act of aggression against Poland in September 1939.

The 'Hitler myth'

Hitler's economic and foreign-policy successes were brilliantly advertised by Goebbels' Propaganda Ministry. The propagation of the 'Hitler myth' which Goebbels masterminded was not concerned with the potentially difficult task of turning Germans into Nazi fanatics, for Hitler's achievements could be explained in terms which would gain the approval of most Germans, with the more questionable aspects of the regime being swept under the carpet. (It is no accident that most of the more dubious, including criminal, aspects of the regime were either committed in secret or outside Germany.) During the 1930s, Goebbels' function was to obtain the consensus and unity of the German people and to promote the illusion of a nation enthusiastically implementing the will of the *Führer*. During the 1940s, as economic and social conditions deteriorated as a

Although mass rallies were organised and controlled for propaganda purposes it is clear there was genuine enthusiasm for Hitler at this women's rally in 1937.

result of the war, the emphasis was on maintaining people's morale and manipulating their emotions (particularly their feelings of fear and terror), in order to prevent the collapse of the Nazi state. Goebbels was successful in these aims, for despite Germany's almost continuous military defeats after 1942 there is little evidence of any internal revolt against the Nazi state. The 'July Plot' of 1944 – the attempted *coup d'état* led by Claus von Stauffenberg and other army officers which failed to kill Hitler and overthrow the Nazi regime – can be said to have been an isolated act of resistance which did not reflect public hostility to the regime. The 'Hitler myth' would remain relatively untarnished until Hitler's suicide in his Berlin bunker on 30 April 1945 ushered in the final days of the Nazi regime.

In fact, for much of the time between 1933 and 1945, it can be argued that Hitler was a popular ruler. Goebbels was highly successful in projecting the 'Hitler myth', both in separating the supposed omnipotence and brilliance of the *Führer* from the sins of the NSDAP and in achieving the gradual acceptance of Nazi radical ideals by much of the German public. Most Germans applauded Hitler's foreign-policy achievements, which made them ready to turn a blind eye to the more brutal aspects of the Nazi regime. The willing accomplices to so many of the wartime atrocities – the legions of military and SS men, the bureaucratic pen-pushers and organisers who, through the conscious use of euphemisms like the 'Final Solution' (*Endlösung*) of the 'Jewish problem', were implicated in so many deaths – stand as testament to the efficacy of the infiltration and acceptance of Nazi values in German society.

As far as the use of terror and the creation of the repressive apparatus of a totalitarian state are concerned, the more criminal aspects of the Nazi regime should be re-examined. While the SS in particular indeed played a sinister role, especially in the occupied territories, the omnipotence and reputation of the Gestapo needs to be reassessed. The evidence suggests that much of the work of the Gestapo was dependent on the active collusion and testimonies of many Germans, who informed on members of their families, friends and neighbours often for the most personal of motives. While a policy of creating fear and repression no doubt helped to cement the Nazification of the 'history of everyday life' in Hitler's Germany, the evidence suggests that the majority of Germans had, for whatever motives, tacitly accepted the legitimacy of the regime and passively (sometimes also actively) supported at least some of its goals.

The meaning of Nazism

The attempted implementation of core aspects of Nazi ideology led directly to the premature deaths of more than 30 million Europeans (probably 20 million Soviet citizens died). These deaths were neither accidental nor the consequence of a radicalisation of policy resulting from the competition of bureaucracies which were eager to influence the *Führer* (although the latter factor may explain the means by which the policy of genocide was often put into practice). Racism was the central myth which provided the dynamic focus of the Nazi regime; it was linked to a tradition of German anti-Semitism and nationalism which can be traced back to the nineteenth century.

Nazi racial doctrines

Although the views of Hitler, as the linchpin and ultimate arbiter of the Nazi system, were the most important single element in the development of Nazi policy, he was far from being the only instigator of the formulation of the aims and implementation of the ideals of the 'racial state' (Burleigh and Wippermann).[3] The most significant of these aims and ideals were *völkisch* nationalism, social Darwinism, anti-Semitism, the quest for *Lebensraum* and the function of war as providing the means by which both national unity could be forged and alleged enemies 'eradicated'. It is a mistake to regard Nazi racism as a policy that was set in stone, for it was constantly evolving and subject to many influences. These included the fanatical anti-Semitism of both the Nazi ideologist Alfred Rosenberg and Hitler (even if, for long periods, mainly for tactical reasons, all references to Jews were absent from Hitler's speeches and directives); Himmler's brand of Nordic mystical racism; the pseudo-scientific justification for ethnic cleansing and population transfers by Nazi academic racists and planning 'experts'; and the '*Blut und Boden*' ('Blood and Soil') theories of Walther Darré (the Nazi minister of agriculture), all of which were part of a ragbag of bizarre racial doctrines.

At the core of the Nazi vision of Germany's national 'rebirth' was a hierarchy of racial 'value', which differentiated between those whom the Nazis judged should be nurtured by the state ('Aryan' people) and the 'useless eaters' who should be denied resources. This latter group included Sinti and Roma people (Gypsies), homosexuals, those in mental institutions, the incurably ill and Jews. (The Nazi's political enemies, particularly communists and socialists, were often conveniently ascribed Jewish ancestry.) For the purposes of international comparison, the Nazis placed Germans and people of predominantly 'Aryan' or 'Nordic' nations at the apex of the racial hierarchy. Beneath them were other European 'races', such as those of Mediterranean and Alpine 'stock', which were ascribed some 'value'. Slavs were deemed 'sub-human' by the Nazis, while

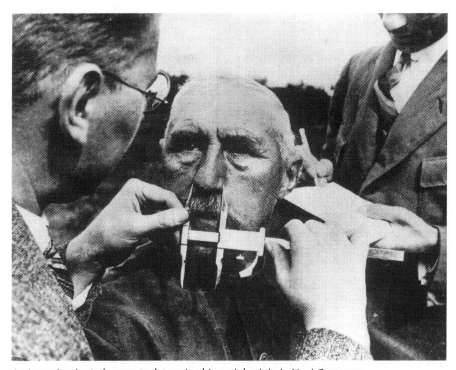

An 'examination' of a man to determine his racial origin in Nazi Germany.

negroid and aboriginal 'races' were alleged to have more in common with monkeys than humans. Jews were said by the Nazis to be the products of 'racial bastardisation', racial mixtures which supposedly threatened humanity by diluting its racial stock and were thus regarded as being inherently 'anti-nature'. The Nazis ascribed spurious physical and psychological characteristics to each race. Aryans, for example, were supposedly tall, blond and blue eyed and possessed the qualities of nobility, heroism and chivalry. Jews, on the other hand, were supposedly hook nosed and evil and possessed a malign intelligence that was bent on world domination. By ascribing 'good' and 'evil' attributes to the different 'races', the Nazis evolved the theory of the need to fight an Apocalyptic 'final battle', with the forces of light (the Aryans) ranged against those of darkness (the Jews).

These were extremely eccentric views, but that they must be taken seriously is demonstrated by the history of the Third Reich. The fact that the barbarous practices of Nazi racism were carried out in secret should not detract from the general culpability of the German people for the Nazis' criminal behaviour during the Second World War. The statistics are horrifying.

1 Between 6 and 7 million Jews died in the Holocaust, euphemistically termed the 'Final Solution' of the 'Jewish problem'.
2 At least 10 million Slavs died as a result of Operation Barbarossa, the Nazi invasion of the Soviet Union which began in June 1941.
3 Over 60 per cent (at least 2 million) of Soviet prisoners of war died in captivity during the Second World War, the great majority being allowed to starve to death.
4 At least 500,000 Gypsies were murdered, while 6,000 children died as a result of 'mercy killing' and 70,000 mentally disabled and senile inhabitants of institutions died as a result of 'disinfections' in the adult 'euthanasia' programme.
5 An estimated 7.7 million foreign forced labourers worked in Germany during the war, and many perished. They had become an indispensable part of the work force in Germany after 1942 and were subject to the same Nazi hierarchy of racial 'value', which determined how they were treated. French labourers, for example, received similar food rations to Germans; Polish and Russian workers were given less; while Jews, political prisoners and concentration-camp inmates were literally worked to death on scientifically calculated minimum diets.

The horrendous, destructive racism of Nazism was implemented as a 'necessary' first step towards creating a 'new order'. For Germans, the 'positive' side of Nazi racism can be seen in the 'stud farms' of the *Lebensborn* experiment, a human-breeding programme by which members of the SS sired 'racially pure' children. The German population furthermore benefited from the vast amount of booty expropriated from conquered territories; from positive social-welfare programmes; and from the Nazi reluctance to cut civilian Germans' living standards during the war or to increase the German female-participation ratio in the workforce.

Racism was a core ideology that drove Nazi policy. In retrospect, the Holocaust, in its attempted genocide of European Jews, appears an act of insanity and evil which is made even more incomprehensible by the top priority given to its implementation from 1944, even as the Nazi edifice was collapsing. The Nazi state's racial policy progressed radically, from anti-Semitic discrimination (1933) to the racist Nuremberg Laws by which marriage between Jews and Aryans was forbidden (1935) to a state-sponsored pogrom (*Kristall-nacht*, 1938) to forcing the Jews to emigrate and formulating the Madagascar Plan (1938–39), by which Jews would be resettled on Madagascar, to the creation of Jewish ghettos in Poland (1940–41) and to the murderous activities of the SS *Einsatzgruppen* (task forces) during the invasion of the USSR. Whether this was a planned strategy seems doubtful (it has all the hallmarks of ad hoc improvisation), but the essential point is that the circumstances of the war made the murder of millions of Jews, Slavs, communists and others who were deemed 'asocial' by the state a logical outcome of Nazi racism.

Although there is believed to be no written '*Führer* order' for the implementation of the Holocaust, the grisly mechanics of the process are clear enough. The decision to implement the 'Final Solution' appears to have been finally taken by Hitler and communicated to Himmler immediately prior to the invasion of the Soviet Union, as British radio intercepts of SS *Einsatzgruppen* messages to Berlin confirm the systematic slaughter of Jews by firing squads from the outset of Operation Barbarossa, set in motion on 22 June 1941. As the enormity of the task became apparent, fears regarding the psychological effects that committing mass murder would have on those members of the SS, *Wehrmacht* and German police who were directly or indirectly involved and worries about the form that enemy propaganda would take if such a policy became public knowledge, more 'efficient' methods of killing were sought. Such worries had also surfaced in Poland, when an increased fear of the transmission of disease to German troops and police by starving Jews in the ghettos in early 1941 put pressure on planners to find the 'Final Solution' to the 'Jewish problem'. The implications of this were spelled out by Reinhard Heydrich, Himmler's deputy, using euphemistic language, at the Wannsee Conference in Berlin in January 1942. While mass shootings of Jews by the *Einsatzgruppen* and their fascist collaborators in the USSR continued, death 'factories', or extermination camps, were established in Poland, first in Operation Reinhard in 1942 (using the gas chambers and personnel that had been employed in Germany from 1938 in the Nazis' secret 'euthanasia' programme) at Chelmno, Belzec, Sobibor and Treblinka. A larger extermination camp was then built at Auschwitz, which superseded the earlier camps, which were closed down by 1943. The Nazis gave top priority to the transportation of Jews from all over Europe to Auschwitz, even when it was obvious that the war was lost.

Structuralist historians, like Hans Mommsen and Martin Broszat,[4] have revealed the chaotic manner in which such genocidal policies were implemented, while intentionalist historians, like Lucy Dawidowicz,[5] have explained why such acts occurred. However, the intentionalist–structuralist argument over whether the Holocaust followed a planned blueprint or was the result of a wartime 'emergency' should not be allowed to mask the criminal and insane nature of the 'Final Solution' in the 'eradication' of racial 'enemies' and 'asocial' groups.

The impact of Nazism

While the horrendous crimes of the Nazis are indisputable, the extent to which Nazi ideas permeated German society and influenced people's behaviour is more problematic. The evidence suggests that Nazi indoctrination was more extensive than many Germans care to remember. Certainly, the lack of any concerted political resistance to Nazism was not due to the supposed omnipotence of the Gestapo, whose alleged efficiency was a myth. The terror instilled in Germans by the Gestapo arose primarily from the fear of denunciation and not from the political surveillance of an overstretched and under-resourced organisation. Evidence from German soldiers' letters home from the Eastern Front suggests that Nazi indoctrination regarding the 'Asiatic hordes' of Bolshevism was faithfully duplicated (although the German army's policy of censorship makes the letters a somewhat tainted source).

Christopher Browning's[6] researches have shown that it was not only members of the SS and *Wehrmacht* who were implicated in mass murder on the Eastern Front: for example, 'ordinary', middle-aged police reservists from Hamburg were involved in the mass murder of the Jews of Jozefow in Poland in 1942. Peer conformity rather than the influence of Nazi doctrine was probably the chief motivation of the majority of those who colluded with the Nazis.

Nazism was simultaneously a barbaric and a modernising force, on the one hand responsible for the most horrific deeds that have ever been committed in European history and, on the other, for the creation of technologically sophisticated fighting machines (a dual truth which is well encapsulated by the image of the V1 and V2 rockets built at Peenemünde by forced labour).

Nazism differed from many other forms of fascism in terms of its resort to mass murder and the extent of its criminal behaviour. Yet while many Italians ignored the order of Mussolini to assist the Nazis in the 'Final Solution', other fascists and ultra-nationalists collaborated with the Nazis during the Second World War. Indeed, many such groups were accused of being more Nazi than the Nazis in their virulent and murderous anti-Semitism (and with reason, particularly in the Ukraine and the Baltic states). It was furthermore not only fascists who collaborated with the Nazi plans for the 'resettlement of Jews in the East', as the Nazis euphemistically termed the Holocaust: the Vichy regime of France, for example, sent all foreign Jews from the 'free zone' (the 'non-occupied' zone under the control of Pétain between 1940 and 1942 but still nominally under his jurisdiction between 1942 and 1944) to Poland.

The Nazis may have been the most radical fascists, but they were not the only racist fascists. Italian Fascism, for example, fought its Abyssinian campaign along racist lines and became anti-Semitic in 1938, but even so, it was not exclusively focused on exterminating its imaginary racial enemies.

Aspects of the Nazi state

4.1 An impression of a Nazi rally, 1932

The April sun shone hot like in summer and turned everything into a picture of gay expectation. There was immaculate order and discipline, although the police left the whole square to the stewards and stood on the sidelines. Nobody spoke of Hitler, always just 'the *Führer*', 'the *Führer* says', 'the *Führer* wants', and what he said and wanted seemed right and good. The hours passed, the sun shone, expectations rose . . . Aeroplanes above us. Testing of the loudspeakers, buzzing of the cine-cameras. It was nearly 3 p.m. 'The *Führer* is coming!' A ripple went through the crowds. Around the speaker's platform one could see hands raised in the Hitler salute . . . A second speaker welcomed Hitler and made way for the man who had drawn 120,000 people of all classes and ages. There stood Hitler in a simple black coat and looked over the crowd, waiting – a forest of swastika pennants swished up, the jubilation of this moment was given vent in a roaring salute.

Source: Frau Luise Solmitz, quoted in J. Noakes and G. Pridham (eds.), *Nazism, 1919–45*, vol. 1, *The rise to power, 1919–34*, Exeter, 1983, p. 74

4.2 The view of the Königsberg *Gau* propaganda chief, 1932

The cause of this decrease [in votes in East Prussia] is to be sought in the events of 1 August [1932]. The acts of terror, which were executed systematically in the entire province, have, through their lack of success and the almost childish manner in which they were carried out, repelled the population from us. Our opponents on all sides have cleverly understood how to make full use of this in their propaganda. In the last 14 days before the elections in all the larger towns in the province special courts were set up which investigated the acts of terror. The reports of the special court proceedings were supplied with venomous commentary in the press of our opponents and were the best means to frighten from us the fickle bourgeois who previously voted for us.

Source: Joachim Paltzo, quoted in R. Bessel, *Political violence and the rise of Nazism*, London, 1984, p. 93

4.3 The view of Hitler's deputy, 1936

How tremendous indeed are the achievements of the new *Reich* in the economic sphere alone! . . . How significant it was to take over a state which, in January 1933, stood on the brink of collapse, with an economy which should, realistically, have long since declared itself bankrupt, and then within the shortest space of time, by means of this state and this economy, to bring about the recovery, to bring millions back into work and bread, to build up a modern army and at the same time as these mighty efforts to secure bread for our people! . . . We are prepared – in the future too – if need be, to consume a little less fat now and then, a little less pork, a few less eggs, because we know that this small sacrifice signifies a sacrifice on the altar of the freedom of our *Volk* [people]. We know that the foreign exchange that we save by so doing goes to benefit rearmament. The slogan 'guns instead of butter!' still holds true today. The *Führer* is not one to do things by halves. Because a world under arms has forced us to rearm, we are rearming fully: each new piece of artillery, each new tank, each new aeroplane means increased certainty for the German mother that her children will not be murdered in an unholy war.

Source: Rudolf Hess, on the 'fats crisis', *Völkischer Beobachter*, 13 October 1936, translated by S. B. Steyne, quoted in N. Frei, *National socialist rule in Germany. The* Führer *state, 1933–45*, Oxford, 1993, pp. 163–64

4.4 Hitler's foreign-policy objectives

The acquisition of land and soil as the objective of our foreign policy and ii) the establishment of a new and uniform foundation as the objective of our domestic policy in accordance with our *völkisch* doctrine . . . The demand for the restoration of the frontiers of 1914 is a political absurdity of such proportions and implications as to make it appear a crime. Apart from anything else, the *Reich*'s frontiers in 1914 were anything but logical. In reality they were neither final in the sense of embracing all ethnic Germans, nor sensible with regard to geo-military considerations.

Thus we National Socialists have intentionally drawn a line under the foreign policy of pre-war Germany. We are taking up where we left off six-hundred years ago. We are putting an end to the perpetual German march towards the South and West of Europe and turning our eyes towards the land in the East. We are finally putting a stop to the colonial and trade policy of the pre-war period and passing over to the territorial policy of the future.

Source: Adolf Hitler, *Mein Kampf*, quoted in J. Noakes and G. Pridham (eds.), *Nazism, 1919–45*, vol. 3, *Foreign policy, war and racial extermination*, Exeter, 1988, p. 615

4.5 The view of the head of the police force

We must be clear about the fact that our opponent in this war is not an opponent in a military sense, but also an ideological opponent. If I speak of an opponent I mean of course our natural enemy, international Bolshevism, led by Jews and Freemasons . . . We must be clear about the fact that Bolshevism is the organisation of subhumanity, is the absolute underpinning of Jewish rule, is the absolute opposite of everything worthwhile, valuable and dear to an Aryan nation. It is a diabolical doctrine because it appeals to the meanest and lowest instincts of mankind and turns them into a religion. Make no mistake: Bolshevism, with its Lenin lying in state in the Kremlin, only needs a few more decades and then this diabolical religion of destruction, based in Asia, will be the religion for the destruction of the whole world. One must also remember that this Bolshevism is planning the Bolshevisation of other nations and in fact this destruction is aimed at the white man.

Source: Heinrich Himmler, lecture to *Reichswehr* officers, January 1937, 'The nature and task of the SS and the police', quoted in J. Noakes and G. Pridham (eds.), *Nazism, 1919–45*, vol. 2, *State, economy and society, 1933–39*, Exeter, 1984, p. 515

4.6 The Nazis' treatment of the Lithuanian Jews

October 30. Again (10.28) 10,000 people have been taken out of the ghetto to die. They selected the old people, mothers with their children, those not capable of working. There were many tragedies: there were cases where a husband had been in town and on his return he no longer found either his wife or his four children! And there were cases where they left the wife and took away the husband. Eyewitnesses tell the tale: on the previous day there was an announcement that everybody must come at six in the morning to the big square in the ghetto and line up in rows, except workers with the documents which were recently distributed to specialists and foremen . . . Some of them were directed to the right – that meant death – and some were directed to the left . . . Nobody suspected that a bitter fate awaited them . . . At dawn there was a rumour that at the ninth fort (the death fort) prisoners had been digging deep ditches, and when the people were taken there it was already clear to everybody that this was death. They broke out crying, wailed, screamed. Some tried to escape on the way there but they were shot dead. Many bodies remained in the fields. At the fort the condemned were stripped of their clothes, and in groups of three hundred they were forced into the ditches. First they threw in the children. The women were shot at the edge of the ditch, after that it was the turn of the men . . . many of whom were covered with earth while they were still alive . . . All the men doing the shooting were drunk. I was told all this by an acquaintance who heard it from a German soldier, an eyewitness, who wrote to his Catholic wife: 'Yesterday I became convinced that there is no God. If there were, He would not allow such things to happen'.

Source: from the diary of a Lithuanian woman doctor on the Jews in the Kovno ghetto, 1941, quoted in Y. Arad, Y. Gutman and A. Margoliat (eds.), *Documents on the Holocaust*, Oxford, 1981, pp. 405–6

Document case-study questions

1 What do 4.1 and 4.2 tell us about the German public reaction to the rise of Nazism?

2 What do 4.3 and 4.4 tell us about the foreign-policy objectives of Nazism?

3 What do 4.5 and 4.6 tell us about Nazi anti-Semitism?

4 What do the sources tell us about the nature of Nazism?

Notes and references

1 Henry Ashby Turner, *Hitler's thirty days to power, January 1933*, London, 1996.

2 Hans Mommsen, *From Weimar to Auschwitz*, Oxford, 1991.

3 M. Burleigh and W. Wippermann, *The racial state: Germany, 1933–45*, Cambridge, 1991.

4 M. Broszat, *The Hitler state*, London, 1981.

5 L. Dawidowicz, *The war against the Jews*, New York, 1986.

6 C. R. Browning, *The path to genocide*, Cambridge, 1992.

5 Other forms of fascism

Although the rise to power of Mussolini in Italy and Hitler in Germany made fascism an important feature of inter-war politics, and the subsequent world war which was fought by the Allies against the fascist imperialist powers and their allies was of immense significance, fascism as a doctrine and movement failed to make a breakthrough in any country other than Italy and Germany. Fascist organisations like the Arrow Cross Party in Hungary and the Iron Guard in Romania had a significant influence on their countries but lacked the sort of mass support that the Nazis enjoyed in Germany.

In spite of economic instability during the inter-war period, the established political democracies of western and northern Europe managed to deflect the threat of political extremism in the forms of both revolutionary communism and the 'alternative revolution' of fascism. In southern and eastern Europe, where fledgling political democracies established after the First World War failed they were replaced by authoritarian, monarchical or military dictatorships, not by communism or the revolutionary nationalism of fascism. Outside Italy and Germany fascists lacked the political space in which to develop, were unable to build a mass base within a democratic structure and were persecuted, marginalised or co-opted (and sometimes all three) by right-wing, authoritarian rulerships. Although Mussolini wavered between proclaiming 'Fascism is not for export' and establishing the Italian leadership of the 'Fascist International', Hitler actively discouraged other forms of fascism, except as 'fifth columns' that could be exploited for Nazi ends, as he perceived foreign revolutionary nationalists as having aims opposed to Nazi and German interests. Yet fascism as a phenomenon cannot be properly understood without some appreciation of the failed forms of fascism, as they illustrate the variety and permutations of fascist doctrine, as well as the complexity of various fascist movements.

Fascism: the stillborn revolution

The First World War created the political and economic instability and the sense of systemic crisis which led to the emergence of fascism. It was the triumph of Mussolini in Italy during the 1920s and, more particularly, the spectacular success of Nazism during the 1930s, however, which encouraged the emergence of populist, revolutionary, nationalist movements throughout Europe, which copied, mimicked or parodied the Italian and German prototypes.

Fascism in France, Spain and Portugal

Mussolini's rise to power was the inspiration behind several fascist movements, like George Valois' *Le Faisceau* ('The Fasces') in France, a serious attempt to emulate Italian Fascism and literally a national socialist movement, and Rotha Lintorn Orman's British Fascisti (after 1924 Fascists), an odd mixture of Colonel Blimp-type figures, right-wing students and blue-shirted thugs, which was viewed by the state with ridicule and distaste and by the security authorities (MI5 and Special Branch) as a cheap source of intelligence (though some of it was inaccurate) about right- and left-wing extremism. Orman's knowledge of Italian Fascism was minimal, but she admired the ruthless tactics which Mussolini's squads had used to destroy the threat of revolutionary communism in Italy.

If the British Fascists could be said to have resembled little more than macho conservatives in fancy dress, *Le Faisceau* was more interesting. Although its name was the French form of the name of Mussolini's *'fasci'*, it developed from a French political tradition. Valois had been an instigator of the discussions between the young group from the extreme-right *Action Française* formed by Charles Maurras and the revolutionary syndicalists of Georges Sorel in the *Cercle Proudhon* movement in 1911. Zeev Sternhell[1] has demonstrated that most of the elements of French fascism had also germinated in French political culture before 1914.

Opposed by both the parliamentary right and much of the radical right, neither *Le Faisceau* nor the British Fascists found the political space in which to develop, due to the relative stability of the prevailing liberal political traditions in France and Britain and the fact that both countries had emerged victorious from the First World War and were therefore not beset by a post-war crisis similar to that which Germany experienced.

It was the 'devil's decade' of the 1930s which led to the mushrooming of fascist movements. The success of Hitler in particular led to an increased Nazi influence on most fascist movements during the second half of the 1930s, although southern European fascist movements appeared more prone to borrow from Italian Fascism. All forms of fascism developed from national cultural traditions and exhibited a wide variety of traits. Some synthesised elements that were more characteristic of the extreme right into their form of fascism. In France, the *Croix de Feu* ('Cross of Fire'), which was founded by Colonel François de la Rocque in 1927 as a veterans' movement and became a uniformed para-fascist organisation in 1936, was banned in the same year by the Blum popular-front government. Its successor, the parliamentary party the *Parti Social Français*, grew to comprise a membership of nearly 1 million in 1938. The *Parti Social Français* was populist, authoritarian and ultra-nationalist and believed in national 'rebirth', but failed either to break out of the mould of radical-right politics or to undermine the parliamentary right, as was demonstrated by the way in which it was prepared to be absorbed into the party-political system instead of pursuing a revolutionary path to power. For their parts, more authentic French fascist movements, like Marcel Bucard's *Francistes* and Jacques Doriot's *Parti Populaire*

Français (PPF), failed to develop an adequate power base with which to threaten the political status quo.

In Spain, although there was a merging in 1934 of the authentic fascist groups the *Juntas de Ofensiva Nacional Sindicalista* (JONS), founded by Ramiro Ledesma Ramos in 1931, and the *Falange*, founded in 1933 by José Antonio Primo de Rivera, they failed to gain more than 2 per cent of the vote in elections during the 1930s. The nationalist right was divided between the republicans, two kinds of monarchists (the Alfonsines and Carlists, each of which supported a rival claimant to the Spanish throne) and militarists, and was Catholic, elitist and dominated by a reactionary landlord class. Tactically, it was also disunited, although the outbreak of the Spanish Civil War in 1936 in any case ruled out a constitutional path to power. After the nationalist leader, General Francisco Franco, defeated the republicans in 1939, he turned Spain into a one-party state, the party concerned comprising fascists and other right-wing factions. The Franco-sponsored *Falange* which resulted did not create an 'alternative revolution' but was instead subordinated to Franco. Franco was content to reinforce traditional conservative and Catholic values within a police state while simultaneously trying to modernise the economy by using a contradictory mixture of neo-corporatism and laissez-faire economics. Although Franco developed a brutal dictatorship between 1939 and 1975, it cannot be said to have been fascist, and it furthermore progressively shed any fascist trappings that it may have had after 1941, when the war turned against Hitler.

From 1932, Portugal also saw the emergence of an authoritarian regime under the prime minister, Dr António de Oliveira Salazar, following the military dictatorship of General António Carmona. Although the Salazar regime copied the style of fascism during the 1930s, with its one-party state, mass rallies and secret-police force, Salazar crushed the authentically fascist National Syndicalist Party led by Rolão Preto in 1934 after a failed revolt. As the prospect of an Axis victory evaporated during the 1940s, Portugal, like Spain, became a reactionary, right-wing, conservative, Catholic and authoritarian nation, whose leader was determined to maintain the privileges of the elite and to preserve the slowly decaying Portuguese empire.

Fascist ideologies

Other forms of fascism developed cultural idiosyncrasies which gave several of them unique characteristics. In Romania, for example, the Iron Guard, founded by Corneliu Codreanu in 1930, was characterised by a type of mystical, pseudo-Christian fascism. The Iron Guard had developed from the paramilitary terrorist group the Legion of the Archangel Michael, so called because Codreanu claimed that he had been directed to form it in a dream in which the archangel appeared to him in 1927. Like the Scythe Cross Party (*Kaszáskereszt*) and Arrow Cross Party (*Nyilaskereszt*) in Hungary, Romanian fascism was notable for its virulent anti-Semitism as, indeed, were most eastern European fascist and ultra-nationalist movements, such as the Fire Cross Party (*Ugunkrust*), later the Thunder Cross Party (*Perkonkrust*), in Latvia, the Iron Wolf Party in Lithuania and the *Vabadussõ*

Sir Oswald Mosley inspects a group of female members of the British Union of Fascists in 1936. Why did fascism fail to become a mass movement in Britain?

jalaste Liit (VAPS) in Estonia. Others, like *Le Faisceau* and the *Falange*, were not anti-Semitic. Like the Italian Fascists, Léon Degrelle's Rexist Party in Belgium and Sir Oswald Mosley's British Union of Fascists (BUF) became increasingly anti-Semitic, either under the influence of Nazism or as a response to Jewish opposition to them.

Some French fascist groups, as well as the BUF, were opposed to their countries fighting a 'brothers' war' against Germany and used pacifist arguments against their nations' involvement in the Second World War, evoking the memory of the horrific slaughter of soldiers of the First World War. Despite their aversion to fighting the Nazis, all fascist movements had a distinctly militaristic and male-chauvinistic ethos. The BUF went out of its way to appeal to women, however, and its separate women's movement, which emphasised equal pay for equal work, recruited several former suffragettes to its ranks. Some forms of fascism were more concerned with defining the relationship between the state, industry and labour, in the way that Mussolini had done. Some fascist movements were more corporatist than others, while others were either more concerned with monetary reform or else were extremely vague about economic policy. In contrast, Mosley and the BUF, which he formed in 1932, developed a coherent, if somewhat Utopian, economic programme based on a pragmatic response to the collapse of the capitalist economy during the 1930s.

While all fascist movements were virulently anti-Marxist, they were equally scathing about what they called 'degenerate' liberalism and 'decadent' bourgeois society and demanded an 'alternative revolution' to that projected by the communists. The many varieties of fascism were most visibly demonstrated by the proliferation of coloured uniforms that distinguished the groups. The black shirts worn by Mussolini's squads, for example, were copied by Mosley's BUF; blue shirts were worn by members of the *Falange* and the Irish paramilitary movement, Eoin O'Duffy's National Guard, whose hard-core members were fascists; green shirts bedecked members of the Hungarian Arrow Cross Party; while grey shirts were worn by Lithuanian fascists.

Fascist membership

European fascist movements attracted people from a wide variety of social classes and backgrounds. Although fascism did attract more than its fair share of abnormal members – cranks, misfits, eccentrics, thugs, criminals, authoritarian personalities, anti-Semites and petty-bourgeois intellectuals – it also recruited a much broader type of personality from across the entire social spectrum. In eastern Europe, fascist movements recruited from the poorest ranks of the peasantry and working classes in a political environment in which the revolutionary left had been outlawed and the reformist left had been manipulated by the political establishment to act as a sort of political 'safety valve'. In France, too, the *Parti Populaire Français*, which was led by former communists, had working-class fascists among its membership. The BUF had a pronounced working-class membership in the East End of London but also recruited alienated conservatives from the middle class between 1932 and 1934, as well as lower-middle-class shopkeepers and pacifists during the second half of the 1930s. While Anton Mussert's Dutch National Socialist Party (*Nationaal Socialistische Beweging*) was predominantly middle class, with a middle-aged profile, most fascist parties prided themselves on their youthful members and their dynamic form of political activism.

Fascist parties appealed to many people who had past military experience or found it difficult to adjust to peacetime conditions after the First World War. Fascism also attracted alienated intellectuals and politicians. Those who felt marginalised and those who experienced considerable frustration about the lack of social change in the depressed conditions of the inter-war period, as well as those who suffered delusions about the pace and scale of modernisation in southern, central and eastern Europe, were also drawn to fascism. While most fascist movements recruited disproportionately from middle- and lower-middle-class groups, their propaganda claims that fascism represented a cross-section of their nations were often not entirely without foundation.

Fascist-style movements and parties recruited most successfully in Austria, Hungary, Romania and Spain. In the last case, the large majority of 'physical-force' nationalists (those who believed in a revolutionary uprising to destroy democracy) upheld traditional, if not reactionary, conservative, Catholic values rather than wanting to effect an 'alternative revolution', even if Franco misleadingly called his one-party state 'Falangist' (the *Falange* was a genuinely fascist party, although its leader, José Antonio Primo de Rivera, disowned the label). Elsewhere, fascists were generally marginalised, and even when they did enter the electoral political arena they very rarely attained more than a few percentage points of the vote. In Iceland, Sweden, Denmark, Norway and the Irish Free State they were not even popular enough to achieve those. Despite its claim to be a constitutional political party, the BUF never fielded a candidate in a parliamentary general election and only ever had one local councillor elected, at Eye, in Suffolk, during the 1930s. In France, the fascist parties formed part of the anti-parliamentary radical right in France.

Fascism in Europe was primarily significant because of the success of Hitler and the Nazis, while Mussolini, despite his inability to transform Italian society, remained in power for 20 years. All the other forms of fascism failed, however, usually miserably.

The failure of fascism

The inability of fascism to develop as a significant political force outside Italy and Germany during the inter-war period was due to a number of factors. One was the collapse of the central European banking system and of international trade during the 1930s, which led to economic contraction and deflation. The League of Nations, which had been set up after the First World War, failed to function as an effective international policeman and could not prevent the Italian Fascist and German Nazi use of force with which to take advantage of international anarchy during the inter-war period. It was this second factor which led to the unilateral revision of the 1919 peace settlement by both Italy and Germany, with the Italian invasion of Abyssinia, the Nazi remilitarisation of the Rhineland, the *Anschluss* with Austria and the incorporation of the Sudetenland into the Third Reich, although nationalists in both countries also supported such revisionism. The successes of Italy and Germany indirectly suppressed the development of other national fascist movements.

The tension between acting in their national interests and maintaining an ideological fraternity with the successful fascist movements of Italy and Germany left other countries' fascist movements open to charges of subversion and treachery and meant that their respective countries' authorities often viewed them in a similarly suspicious light as communist parties. In western Europe, the fact that many fascist parties, including the BUF, were not critical of Italian Fascism and German Nazi imperialism during the later 1930s and, indeed, actively campaigned for appeasement and the revision of the 1919 peace treaties, increased the political establishments' suspicion that such domestic fascist parties were a potential 'fifth column'.

In central and eastern Europe, domestic fascist movements were viewed as a subversive revolutionary force in a political environment in which Marxist parties had either been outlawed or allowed a token political representation. In Romania, the Iron Guard was banned by King Carol in 1938 and its leader,

Codreanu, was shot 'while trying to escape' in the same year (thus his 'martyrdom' was added to the mystical, religious aura of Romanian fascism). King Carol and, following his abdication in 1940, General Ion Antonescu (who, after he became prime minister, assumed dictatorial powers), collaborated with, co-opted and then eventually destroyed the Iron Guard between 1938 and 1944. In Hungary, the fascist Gjula Gömbös was President Miklós Horthy's prime minister between 1932 and 1936, but Ferenc Szálasi's radical fascist Arrow Cross Party achieved only token power when Hungary came under German control in 1944.

Fascism failed outside Italy and Germany, both because of its limited electoral appeal before 1939 and because it was tainted by association with the Axis powers during the Second World War. In spite of the collapse of economic and political stability caused by the First World War that characterised the inter-war period, outside Italy and Germany fascism failed to find the political space within which to develop a credible challenge to the unstable political systems which, after 1933, were generally making a slow, if erratic, recovery. The 'fascist revolution' was perceived as unnecessary by most people, particularly after the threat of international communism receded. Fascism was furthermore based on German and Italian traditions and evoked mixed feelings of fear, loathing and ridicule in most societies (understandably, given the examples of Nazi Germany and Fascist Italy).

Fascism re-evaluated

Despite their failure and political insignificance, a good case can be made for the study of national forms of fascism, however. Although they have developed different definitions of fascism, Zeev Sternhell and Roger Griffin[2] have both demonstrated fascism's links with wider cultural and political trends in recent history. Sternhell has emphasised that most of the elements of fascism developed during the French Third Republic between 1871 and 1940 and that fascist ideology was deeply implanted in French culture and intellectual discourse by the 1930s. Griffin has demonstrated the applicability of his own model of fascist ideology to a wide variety of movements in twentieth-century Europe, as well as to some non-European fascist movements and a broad range of ultra-nationalist and neo-fascist thought since 1945, in addition to the 'classical' fascist inter-war period. For Griffin, fascism is seen as a form of national 'rebirth' (palingenesis), a revolutionary movement which wishes to destroy all other political forms and the 'decadence' of contemporary society to create a 'new order' based on the 'new man' with 'new values'. Regardless of its electoral success or failure in individual states, fascism is an important political phenomenon because it represents the response of the extreme right, both to the economic crisis and the threat of Marxist revolution. 'Classical' fascism may have been thought to have been defeated in 1945, but new forms of the phenomenon were to be added to the variety of other forms of fascism.

Fascist doctrines in Belgium, Britain and Romania

5.1 The view of the leader of the Belgian Rexist Party

The intransigence of the new generation will turn them into arsonists or crusaders. They will no longer tolerate half-baked solutions. They will create a new world, a complete social order, a seamless system of justice, a real fraternity among people, a society no longer based on degradation, hatred, the stifling of thought, but on human dignity, on profound virtues, and on the peace which stems from spiritual growth. Our century will either be a century of the soul, or it is doomed to burn like a funeral pyre.

Source: Léon Degrelle, *The revolution of souls*, Paris, 1938, translated by Roger Griffin, in R. Griffin (ed.), *Fascism: a reader*, Oxford, 1995, p. 205

5.2 The view of the leader of the British Union of Fascists

This paper will work for the Fascist revolution. Nothing less than a revolution in our system of government will do today.

Let our position be quite clear. We seek our ends by legal and constitutional means. We hope that the British people will take action in time. We desire to avert the collapse which has led to bloodshed and violence on the Continent. We believe that it is possible to carry out by peaceful means the great changes that must come.

On the other hand, we recognise that things may be allowed to drift too far, and that other methods may thus become necessary. If the present system of Government continues too long, and the present politicians are allowed to muddle along much further, we may reach disaster before action has been taken.

In that event, a different situation will arise for which Fascism must also be prepared. If our present political system muddles to collapse, Fascism alone can stand between the country and anarchy. We must be prepared to save Britain by force from those who seek to destroy her by force.

Source: Sir Oswald Mosley, 'On to Fascist revolution', *Blackshirt 1*, February 1933

5.3 The view of the leader of the Romanian Iron Guard

I will underline this once again: we are not up against a few pathetic individuals who have landed up here by chance and who now seek protection and shelter. We are up against a fully fledged Jewish state, an entire army which has come here with its sights set on conquest. The movement of the Jewish people and its penetration into Romania are being carried out in accordance with precise plans. In all probability the 'Great Jewish Council' is planning the creation of a new Palestine on a strip of land which, starting off in the Baltic Sea, embraces a part of Poland and Czechoslovakia and half of Romania right across to the Black Sea . . . There will come a time when all the peoples of the earth will fight their way through to this final resurrection, all the peoples with their dead leaders. Then each people will be given a special place before the throne of God.

This final act, this overwhelming moment, this resurrection of the dead, is the highest and most sublime goal which a people can aspire to.

Source: Corneliu Codreanu, 'The programme of the Iron Guard', translated from a German translation of the Romanian original by Roger Griffin, in R. Griffin (ed.), *Fascism: a reader*, Oxford, 1995, pp. 221–22

Document case-study questions

1 What similarities and differences are there between these sources and those used to illustrate Italian Fascism and German Nazism?

2 Why do you think fascism was more significant in Romania (5.3) than in either Belgium (5.1) or Britain (5.2)?

3 What features of 'generic fascism' are illustrated by these sources?

4 What do these sources suggest about the motivations of fascists?

Notes and references

1 Z. Sternhell *et al*, *The birth of fascist ideology*, Princeton, 1994.

2 Z. Sternhell *et al*, *The birth of fascist ideology*, Princeton, 1994, and R. Griffin, *The nature of fascism*, London, 1991.

6 Anti-fascism

A 1932 photomontage by the anti-Nazi artist, John Heartfield. The German reads: 'The meaning of the Hitler salute; Millions are backing me; A little man asks for great gifts'. The millions, the picture implies, are the millions of marks provided by capitalist sympathisers, not millions of people, as Hitler meant. Why would this photomontage appeal to Communists?

As a movement, anti-fascism originated as a practical necessity for the revolutionary political left. The Bolshevik Revolution of 1917 and the attempt of its leaders, Lenin and Trotsky, to export it by means of both internal subversion by communists in other countries and the use of the Red Army led to repressive measures being taken by most nations against the activities of the Comintern (the Communist International) in Moscow, the international arm of Soviet communism that controlled non-Soviet communist parties and plotted the downfall of capitalism from 1919 to 1943. Although independent, paramilitary, fascist 'White Guards', as Marxists termed them, such as the *Freikorps* in Germany, the *Heimwehr* ('home guard') in Austria and the Men of Szeged in Hungary, were responsible for violently suppressing communist uprisings after 1918, Soviet and Comintern propaganda became rapidly focused on the mass politics of Italian Fascism during the 1920s and German Nazism during the 1930s, as these regimes developed more systematic forms of repression to destroy all forms of opposition to them, beginning with the ruthless suppression of revolutionary communism.

By redefining Lenin's theory of imperialism, the Comintern portrayed fascism as the highest stage of capitalist development (albeit of an extremely unstable variety), identifying it as an attempt of a desperate ruling class to prevent the victory of the international communist revolution by means of terrorist violence. Josef Stalin, the Soviet leader from 1925, made this supposed threat appear worse by arguing that all those who had not embraced revolutionary communist discipline were aiding the development of fascism in capitalist societies and claiming that reformist socialists were therefore 'social fascists'. Any unified international working-class defence against fascism was, as a result, inevitably undermined, with tragic consequences in Germany between 1930 and 1933. While it was true that the German Social Democratic Party (*Sozialdemokratische Partei Deutschlands*, SPD) and the Communist Party (*Kommunistische Partei Deutschlands*, KPD) were unable to work together after the foundation of the KPD in December 1918, Stalin made matters worse by ordering the KPD to co-operate with the Nazis in bringing down the Weimar democracy. The Comintern's 'about turn' of 1935, which called for working-class unity against fascism, did not improve matters significantly, because although 'popular-front' governments (alliances of communists, liberal democrats and socialists) were elected in France and Spain in 1936, deep-rooted suspicions between reformists and revolutionary socialists ultimately led to the failure of the Spanish Second Republic and the demise of the popular front in France. For many Marxists, the final 'betrayal' occurred in August 1939, when Stalin signed the Nazi–Soviet Pact with Germany and thus effectively ordered all communists to regard Hitler as an ally.

While Italian Fascist and German Nazi revisionism in altering the Treaty of Versailles gave rise to international concern in 1935, their deep suspicion of international communism prevented both authoritarian and democratic governments, as in Britain and France, from placing their trust in the Soviet Union's call for an international policy of 'collective security' to counter incidences of fascist aggression in the east. The breakdown of the international economy and increasing criticism of the Versailles peace settlement in Britain during the inter-war period led to international attempts to appease, rather than oppose, the Italian and German dictators following the failure of the League of Nations to stop the Italian invasion of Abyssinia in 1935. When seen in retrospect, the Munich Agreement (1938), by which Germany was allowed to annexe the Sudetenland, proved that appeasement encouraged aggressive behaviour on the part of fascist dictators; it was only in 1939 that a firm stand was taken against Nazi imperialism. Even then, it took the Nazi invasion of the Soviet Union in June 1941 before the 'grand alliance' between Britain and the Soviet Union, and later the United States, was created against Hitler. (Perhaps not surprisingly, after the German defeat in 1945 this anti-Nazi pact of convenience soon degenerated into the animosity of the Cold War.)

The united and popular fronts against fascism

Anti-fascism as a movement developed as an organised Marxist response to the ruthless liquidation of socialist and revolutionary communist working-class movements by fascist regimes and the incorporation of their membership into fascist-controlled organisations. While capitalist states might have supported the counter-revolutionary activities of reactionary political elites, as was seen in Miklós Horthy's regime in Hungary (Horthy overthrew Béla Kun's communist government in 1919), the emergence of fascism created a more difficult, and increasingly pressing, problem for Lenin and the Bolsheviks in the immediate aftermath of the First World War. Marxist doctrine tended to blame fascism for all forms of right-wing, counter-revolutionary activities after 1918, but rulers like Horthy were not fascists.

The defeat of the communists in Italy at the hands of the Fascist squads of the renegade revolutionary socialist Mussolini led Italian Marxists to debate whether financial, industrial or agrarian capitalists were behind fascism. In the Comintern, Antonio Gramsci and Clara Zetkin pointed out that the distinguishing feature of Italian Fascism which differentiated it from the reactionary right and capitalist elites was its mass support in sections of the peasantry and its appeal to white-collar workers. Fascism, according to the Comintern, had become a reactionary revolution of the *petit-bourgeoisie*, which was being manipulated by agents of monopoly capitalism. Stalin's consolidation of power in the USSR resulted in the elimination of the political right. This development corresponded with the rise of Hitler during the Comintern's 'third period', which saw the Third International not only defining all capitalist states as being incipiently fascist but also all forms of socialist opposition which were not under Stalinist control being branded 'social fascists'. Fascism was regarded by Marxists as representing the death throes of the age of imperialism, the highest stage of capitalist development identified by Lenin.

Divisions in the socialist movement

Irreconcilable divisions in the international socialist movement first emerged during the 1890s with the split between the revisionists (who believed in reforming capitalist structures in order to produce an evolutionary path to socialism) and the revolutionaries (who believed that socialism could be achieved only after the capitalist system had been destroyed). This division became a chasm on the outbreak of the First World War. Most of the revisionists affiliated to the Second International (formed in 1889) had adopted a 'social chauvinist' position on the outbreak of the war and supported their respective national governments. Some of the revolutionaries followed Lenin and the Bolsheviks in campaigning for a policy of 'revolutionary defeatism', arguing against the 'imperialist war'. Mussolini perceived that the official line of the Second International, that of working-class neutrality, did not correspond to reality and that such sentiments of working-class solidarity were less potent than nationalism. Lenin explained this dichotomy in his theory of imperialism, by which, he believed, capitalists had succeeded in bribing the most skilled workers with promises of imperialist profits from outside Europe. The Bolshevik Revolution led to the creation of the Third International in 1919, under the direction of the Comintern (in reality the international arm of the Soviet Union), which formalised the deep divisions between the reformists and revolutionaries within the international socialist movement. The split would have a wider significance: the bitter dispute between the advocates of social democracy, whose supporters rejected revolutionary violence, and those of communism prevented effective co-operation between the parties of the political left, which assisted the rise to power of both Hitler and Mussolini.

'After Hitler, us' said the KPD slogan, but the Nazis did not agree with this prediction. Following the Reichstag fire, a fortuitous event for the Nazis which enabled them to destroy the KPD within weeks of Hitler becoming chancellor in 1933, Hitler put in motion a ruthless policy of the suppression of the entire working-class movement and the incorporation of all potential opponents into fascist bodies. German communists and socialists were either murdered, incarcerated in concentration camps or driven into exile. Even in the final days of their existence the KPD and SPD were divided with regard to tactics: the KPD being intent on following a sectarian revolutionary path and the SPD being determined to avoid giving the Nazis an excuse for suppressing them. Those KPD and SPD leaders who survived blamed each other for the debacle, the outcome of which was the destruction of working-class political movements, the imposition of a police state, the incorporation of German workers into the German Labour Front (*Deutsche Arbeitsfront*, DAF), which replaced the trade unions from 1934, and the indoctrination of the nation with Nazi propaganda orchestrated by Goebbels.

The Reichstag fire and its impact

The Reichstag fire was not only important in heralding the nadir of German working-class politics but also in influencing the transformation of the Comintern's policy regarding fascism. Arrested in Berlin for his alleged role in organising the Reichstag-fire 'conspiracy', the Comintern representative Georgi Dimitrov turned the trial into a farce by showing that there was no evidence to connect the KPD with the Reichstag fire and the court was forced to acquit him. He was deported to the Soviet Union, where he was fêted as a communist hero and was able to convince Stalin of the need for a change of policy, arguing that only an alliance of working-class and progressive political forces could check the menace of fascism.

In Paris, a carefully manipulated propaganda campaign was set in motion by the Comintern's representatives, Willi Münzenberg and Otto Katz, in 1933, and an inquiry into the Reichstag fire was held in both Paris and London to alert progressive political opinion to the dangers of fascism and Nazism. In England, the Communist Party of Great Britain (CPGB) was amongst the first of the national communist parties to emerge from its ultra-left-wing, sectarian phase and actively worked to create a 'united front' with other socialists against fascism. It established a working relationship, based on an anti-fascist platform, with the Independent Labour Party in 1933 and, unofficially, with left-wing elements within the Labour Party.

The popular fronts

In 1934 Stalin sanctioned the tentative beginnings of the popular front in France when Maurice Thorez, the French Communist Party leader, proposed a working alliance with the socialists and other progressive political forces against the threat posed by a potential fascist *coup d'état* following the demonstration of 6–7 February 1934 by members of the *Croix de Feu* and other fascist groups. This was the background to the 'about turn' of the Communist International in 1935, when Dimitrov announced the need for communists to work with other socialists and progressive political forces to oppose fascism. While this was a significant move towards the creation of an anti-fascist movement, the subtext of Dimitrov's speech revealed that little had changed. The emphasis on a communist domination of any such alliance and the consequent inevitable eventual triumph of the Third International did little to allay social democratic and socialist fears that this change of policy was as much a ruse to enable communist infiltration and domination of reformist working-class movements as it was intended to create an anti-fascist alliance (these fears indeed proved the case in Spain, where members of the Soviet secret police, the KGB, and Spanish communists seemed as keen on murdering Trotskyists and anarchists as they were on fighting Franco). The British Labour Party expelled those who co-operated with the CPGB during the inter-war period, while the French socialists, although supported by the communists in the 'popular-front' governments of Léon Blum (1936–38), formed a cabinet without communist representatives.

The failure of 'collective security'

Until the rise of Hitler, states were not officially alarmed by fascism. Mussolini's actions were generally perceived by right-wing governments during the 1920s as having achieved a desirable restoration of law and order in Italy. Mussolini's foreign policy, in which he tried to resolve foreign-policy problems by diplomatic means (despite one or two lapses, such as the invasion of Corfu in 1923), was regarded as that of a 'good European', while his conspicuously enthusiastic endorsement of most of the international declarations of peace, such as the Locarno Treaty of 1925 which guaranteed the borders of Belgium, France and Germany, was viewed with approval. In contrast, Hitler's actions during the 1930s, from leaving the League of Nations (1933) to the rearmament of Germany, the remilitarisation of the Rhineland (1936), the *Anschluss* ('connection') with Austria (1938), the annexation of the Sudetenland region of Czechoslovakia (1938) and the invasion of Poland (1939), caused a change in other countries' attitudes to fascism, particularly after the emergence of the 'brutal friendship' and then the 'Pact of Steel' (1939) between Hitler and Mussolini. Continuing suspicion of the aims and intentions of the Soviet Union, however, resulted in the failure of attempts to create a state of 'collective security', or an anti-fascist alliance, against Nazi imperialism and its revisionist attempts to re-draw the map of Europe. Indifference to fascism thus turned to alarm within most European democracies, and some authoritarian, right-wing regimes, as in Hungary and Romania, began to persecute fascist movements from 1936. It was in Spain in 1936 that the confrontation between fascism and its enemies was to begin, the Spanish Civil War being the forerunner of a larger conflict which was to divide and devastate Europe.

The Spanish Civil War

The Spanish Second Republic, which was formed in 1931, was unstable from the outset. After the collapse of General Miguel Primo de Rivera's military dictatorship in 1930 and the monarchy in 1931, the failure of both the political left and right to establish an effective government in the new republic during the 1930s led to growing anarchy, political violence and acts of terrorism. Anarcho-syndicalists (who believed in the use of the general strike as a revolutionary weapon) resorted to violence against landlords and seized land, murdered priests, raped nuns and burned churches. Communist miners led the revolutionary uprising in Asturias in 1934, which was put down with difficulty by the army. There were also two right-wing conspiracies organised by General Emilio Mola to overthrow Manuel Azaña's left-wing governments: the first was in 1933 and the second developed into the nationalist uprising of 1936 under Francisco Franco's leadership. The Spanish Civil War resulted from the failure of the governments of the republic to maintain the rule of law, as well as from the growth of political extremism.

The European powers and the Spanish Civil War

Somewhat ironically, neither the communists nor the fascists had significant support in Spain. Both the *Juntas de Ofensiva Nacional Sindicalista* (JONS) and the *Falange* were minuscule groups on the extreme right which, even after they merged, obtained only 2 per cent of the popular vote in 1936. Similarly, the Spanish Communist Party played second fiddle to the anarcho-syndicalists on the revolutionary left.

Two significant developments can be said to have turned the Spanish Civil War into the forerunner of the Second World War: communist propaganda to the effect that the nationalist and military uprising of July 1936 was an attempted fascist revolution; and the actions of Mussolini and Hitler in providing military aid to enable Franco to continue the military insurrection and eventually to overthrow the republic in 1939. The failure of the democratic powers' policy of non-intervention, which reflected the appeasement policy of the British and the French government's desire to avoid provoking a civil war in its country, meant that it was left to Stalin to provide the necessary aid to prevent the Spanish popular-front government from collapsing in 1936. Underlying Stalin's unilateral declaration of 'collective security' were more Machiavellian motives than those of altruism or idealism, however, for by providing sufficient aid to the republicans to stiffen their resistance against the nationalists Stalin was able to deflect Nazi aggression from eastern Europe until 1938.

The Nazi and Fascist intervention in the Spanish Civil War was also based on cynical motives, for war-torn Spain became a testing ground for new weapons and methods of warfare, as was symbolised by one of the great masterpieces of twentieth-century art, Pablo Picasso's *Guernica* (1937), which depicted the trauma and tragedy experienced by civilian casualties when the town was destroyed in a bombing raid by the German Condor Legion. As a result of Nazi and Fascist intervention, popular-front propaganda succeeded in portraying the Spanish Civil War as a war against fascism. The heroic exploits of the 'international brigades' (republican sympathisers from Europe and the United States who had volunteered to fight) and the more sinister activities of the Soviet secret police, the NKVD, which seemed more intent on murdering 'Trotskyist' Spanish revolutionaries (Stalin had deported Trotsky from the Soviet Union in 1929) than on fighting Franco, ensured that the significance of Spanish communism as a political force was greatly inflated during the war.

Franco's motivations

Popular-front propaganda was successful in depicting the alliance between the reactionary right and international fascism in Spain as a threat to the security of Europe, and persuaded European public opinion that it was necessary to be firm with dictators. Although the details of the Spanish Civil War are of little importance in a study of the concept of fascism (given that Franco was not a fascist), both communist propaganda and Franco's need to retain the support of the fascist dictators ensured that 'Spanish fascism' became inextricably linked with Franco's nationalist uprising in European public opinion. In fact, Franco was simultaneously a shrewd politician, a reactionary, Catholic, nationalist and a ruthless military dictator who had a strong appreciation of how massacres of civilians could destroy the resistance of conquered populations. Franco had no conception of an 'alternative revolution'; the nationalist uprising which he led was intended to preserve the decaying structures and ethos of a traditional Spain, based on the conservative values of Roman Catholicism as both the state religion and the guardian and interpreter of moral and social values and education. Franco also aimed to preserve the privileges and social power of landowners, as well as the armed forces' and police's role in enforcing discipline and public order. Franco furthermore wanted to extend Spanish influence internationally, but although this aim proved unattainable Francoism was able to enforce its other goals.

The question as to whether or not Franco was a fascist was confused further by the 'shotgun marriage' of the Spanish nationalist right and the fascists in 1937. In a pragmatic political move, Franco adopted the *Falange* and created a single new state party, the *Falange Española Tradicionalista y de las JONS*, a title which reflected the forced merger of the fascist *Falange* with both Alfonsine and Carlist monarchists and elements of the nationalist and republican right. The new party was an ideological mishmash which could be easily manipulated by Franco and the military. Franco's strategy during the Spanish Civil War was to destroy ruthlessly the anti-fascist popular front; his 'politics of revenge' led to the slaughter of 200,000 anti-fascist Spaniards during and after the civil war. Although the new *Falange* may have provided a legalistic gloss for such behaviour, it was not fascist. The party was always under the control of the military, and even if up until 1945 radical right-wing elements did have a certain amount of influence (given Franco's debt to Mussolini and Hitler), Franco's regime came to have more in common with authoritarian and military dictatorships, such as those of Salazar in Portugal, Antonescu in Romania and Horthy in Hungary, than with fascism.

The significance of the Spanish Civil War

It was the international significance of the Spanish Civil War, rather than events in Spain, which proved more important for fascism. The Spanish Civil War displayed the weakness of the anti-fascist movement and demonstrated to Hitler that there was no effective 'collective security' with which to check Nazi expansionism. Although Soviet intervention in the war slowed down Franco's advance significantly, this was as much due to Franco's obsessive strategy of immediately 'cleansing' conquered territory with the liberal application of his 'politics of revenge'.

The fact that Britain and France were reluctant to join forces with the Soviet Union in an anti-fascist crusade was also not lost on Hitler. Similarly, he could not have failed to notice that Britain and France, although united in their policy of non-intervention in Spain, were divided in their motives. Neville Chamberlain's government was concerned about the threat to the balance of power in Europe posed by Hitler, but Britain's lack of preparedness for war, the cost of rearmament, the fear of potential damage to civilians and the perceived justice of Hitler's claim for the need for the revision of some of the more punitive clauses of the Treaty of Versailles were all seen as arguments which supported a policy of appeasement rather than one of standing up to aggression. France was politically divided between the radical-socialist popular-front government (which was backed by the communists), those who supported the Spanish Second Republic and members of the constitutional and radical right, who were vehement in their refusal to back any intervention in the Spanish Civil War on behalf of those whom they regarded as anarcho-syndicalist burners of churches and rapers of nuns.

The failure of 'collective security', both in terms of the League of Nations' inability to act as an effective international policeman and that of Britain and France to co-operate with Stalin during the Spanish Civil War, led Hitler to believe that there was little threat of effective international action hindering his expansionist aims. The forcing of the *Anschluss* with Austria and the acquisition of the Sudetenland (both in 1938), Hitler's supposedly last territorial claims in Europe, demonstrated the difficulties involved in forming an effective alliance against fascist aggression. Although the democracies were to stiffen their resistance to Hitler after the Munich Agreement, the continuing mutual distrust between Britain, France and the Soviet Union enabled Hitler to exploit the failure of 'collective security' and the anti-fascist alliance until the time of Germany's invasion of the Soviet Union on 22 June 1941.

Communist anti-fascist strategies

6.1 The directive of the leader of the Comintern

The defence of the immediate economic and political interests of the working class, the defence of the latter against fascism, must be the starting point and form the main content of the workers' united front in all capitalist countries . . . Communists must not limit themselves to merely issuing appeals to struggle for proletarian dictatorship, but must show the mass what they are to do today to defend themselves against capitalist plunder and fascist barbarity . . . the Communists, in order to render the road to unity of action easier for the workers, must strive to secure joint action with the Social Democratic Parties, reforming trade unions and other organisations of the toilers against the class enemies of the proletariat on the basis of short- or long-term agreements.

Source: Georgi Dimitrov, speech made in 1935 to the Comintern, 'The offensive of fascism and the tasks of the Communist International. The fight for the unity of the working class against fascism'

6.2 The declaration of the British Communist Party, 1934

The Communist Party will therefore support the formation of the anti-fascist front composed of individuals and organisations which are prepared to fight fascism whether expressed in the fight against the hooliganism of the Mosley murder gangs or the legislation of the National Government. Such a movement will drive for the abandoning of the slave labour camps, the withdrawal of the Sedition Bill, against the increased power of the police for public meetings, for the closing down of the Mosley barracks, for the prohibition of the Mosley uniforms and for the dissolution of the Mosley defence corps . . . The Communist Party warns the workers against those who under the plea of 'free speech' are clearing the way for a further development of the fascist movement in this country. Moreover for Mosley to talk of free speech is hypocrisy: it is a clear intention of fascism to suppress the working-class movement in this country and to brutally ill treat and murder its leaders. In addition the recent anti-Semitic drive of Mosley shows that he intends to unloose a movement of anti-Jewish bestiality in this country. The working-class movement having seen fascism at work in Austria and Germany will do all in its power to smash this movement which aims at destroying every working class institution in the interests of monopoly capital.

Source: a British Communist Party declaration, read by J. R. Campbell at an anti-fascist rally in Hyde Park, London, 17 June 1934, quoted in the Public Record Office document PRO HO45/25383/307308

6.3 A statement by the Spanish Communist Party, 1937

In spite of everything, at all cost, we must maintain the Popular Front. Whatever the difficulties which are formed in our path, the Communist Party will continue to be the most vigorous defender of the Popular Front and of its expression in power: the legitimate government . . . Who are the enemies of the People? The enemies of the People are the fascists, the Trotskyists and the 'uncontrollables'. Our principle enemy is fascism; but our hatred is also directed with the same concentrated force against the agents of fascism who hide themselves behind pretended revolutionary slogans as Poumists, disguised Trotskyists, the better to accomplish their mission as agents of our enemies waiting in ambush in our own territory. We cannot annihilate the fifth column without also annihilating those who also defend politically the enemy's slogans directed at disrupting and disuniting the anti-fascist forces.

Source: a Spanish Communist Party statement attacking Trotskyists as 'agents of fascism', 1937

Document case-study questions

1 What does 6.1 tell us about the Comintern's concern about fascism?
2 What does 6.2 tell us about the interpretation of fascism by the Communist Party of Great Britain?
3 What does 6.3 suggest about the reasons for the failure of the popular fronts against Franco?
4 What do these sources tell us about the nature of anti-fascism?

7 The Nazi 'new order'

Fascism was a revolutionary doctrine whose aim was to create a 'new man' and a 'new order' – an aim which remained a fantasy as far as those fascist movements outside Italy and Germany were concerned. Plans for a 'Fascist International' under Italian direction (but boycotted by Hitler) or the carving-up of world resources by a federation of fascist powers in alliance with Japan were not realised during the inter-war period, although the Second World War was seen by some naive fascist idealists as an attempt to implement these dreams. For the Nazis, war was the furnace within which the 'new order' would be forged, the outcome of the struggle between peoples as predicted by the social Darwinian principle of the survival of the fittest. It was the murderous blueprint for 'Nazi selection' rather than that of natural selection which would transform the map of Europe and have profound repercussions over the next 50 years.

The application of a spurious form of 'morality' based on pseudo-scientific, racist principles meant that the Nazis treated the more 'Aryan' populations of western and northern Europe with a certain degree of humanity and that the Geneva Conventions, which laid down rules for the treatment of prisoners of war, were complied with. For the people of eastern Europe and Jews, however, the 'new order' meant enslavement or extermination, resulting in the deaths of over 20 million civilians. Compared with the Nazi exemplar, the Utopian schemes of the abortive fascist movements of the inter-war period or the 'Euro-fascist' ideas which gained ground after 1945 pale into insignificance with regard to their potential for atrocities.

Nazi ideals and plans for its 'new order' were themselves far from coherent, however. Like much of the Nazi system, the implementation of such policies depended as much on local initiatives as central direction, with few clear orders being dictated from on high and a cumulative radicalisation of policy resulting from competing agencies trying to guess what Hitler wanted while they were 'working towards the *Führer*'.

The German invasion of the Soviet Union in 1941 led to the most destructive phase of the 'new order' being put into operation on the Eastern Front, although the destruction of the Polish intelligentsia and the escalation of the separation, deportation and murder of Jews in Poland after September 1939 was a foretaste of what was to come. The invasion enabled the 'resettlement' of the Jews 'in the east' (which rapidly developed into the Holocaust), as well as the murder of at least 60 per cent of the total number of Soviet prisoners of war and the killing through starvation and forced labour of many millions of Europeans who were deemed to be 'inferior' according to Nazi racist criteria. In spite of Goebbels' propaganda, which promised the prospect of a harmonious community of European states under German leadership, the reality of Hitler's conquests was a Nazi hegemony, involving the stealing of booty, the imposition of massive 'reparations' and the restructuring of the conquered countries' economic resources for the benefit of the victors.

The implementation of Nazi racist policies created a hierarchy of nations and peoples, with the 'eradication' of those whom the Nazis classified as being 'without value', particularly outside Germany, including Jews, communists, Gypsies, homosexuals and mentally and physically disabled people. The 'new order' also involved the mass transference of populations across Europe, with most of the Slavs who had survived the Nazi invasion being earmarked for western Siberia, a plan which was never actually implemented due to the circumstances of the war. The Nazi vision was truly horrific in both concept and execution. In practice, the 'new order' became literally a 'revolution of destruction' for countless millions of Europeans and ultimately led to the downfall of the Hitler and his Third Reich.

The 'rebirth' of Europe

The Second World War was fought by Hitler to achieve German hegemony in Europe at the least, if not world domination. The aim was to create the necessary 'living space' (*Lebensraum*) for the German people. Although *Hitler's secret book*[1] in particular appears to give an outline plan of his foreign-policy aims, this, as well as other sources, can only be treated as an ideal intention, as Hitler's long-term goals were usually subordinated to pragmatic possibilities. Hitler's aim was to create an alliance with Italy and Britain, leaving him free to establish a Nazi empire to be created in the states of eastern Europe and the Soviet Union, which he intended to conquer. Hitler, however, like Lenin, was always prepared to take two metaphorical steps backwards in order to take one step forward. The most notorious example of this policy was the Nazi–Soviet Pact of 1939, when Hitler made a temporary alliance with the USSR in order to be free to invade and partition Poland. He then exploited Stalin's neutrality to attack westwards, before reverting to his ideological goal: the invasion of the Soviet Union by means of Operation Barbarossa in 1941.

Hitler's ends were thus ideologically driven, but the means by which they were implemented were flexible, in terms of both diplomatic and military tactics. Hitler's failure to defeat Britain before embarking on the invasion of the Soviet Union and his declaration of war on the United States after the Japanese attack on Pearl Harbor in December 1941 represented a self-destructive policy, however, as Germany embarked on a two-front war from 1941, for the new combination of Germany's enemies could far out-produce Nazi Germany in the manufacturing of munitions. Prior to this mistake, Hitler had brilliantly combined a policy of the diplomatic bullying of a single, weak opponent, like Poland, with the willingness to engage in a rapid *Blitzkrieg* ('lightning war'), although this strategy was forced upon him because Germany was not ready for total war in 1939, as Richard Overy[2] has made clear. This combination of ideological goals, pragmatic flexibility and revolutionary military tactics enabled Hitler temporarily to create a Nazi empire which stretched from Norway's North Cape to the Mediterranean Sea and from the Ural Mountains to the Atlantic seaboard of France by 1942.

The relationship between Nazism and European fascism

For the Nazis, war created the conditions necessary for the survival of the fittest, which in turn forged the qualities of the 'new man', a warrior without fear or pity. War, according to the Nazi viewpoint, was not only ideologically desirable, being the crucible from which such new values would be produced, but further-more represented an essential step in humankind's evolution towards a higher form. This was a commonplace view which was held by many European fascists, the corollary being that those who opposed a fascist war or who fought against Hitler were effectively propping up the 'decadent' international order and were thereby risking the potential destruction of Europe as it became a prey to the 'Asiatic hordes' of Bolshevism and the economic power of the American dollar.

A policy of dwelling on the potentially destructive alternatives to fascism underlay Goebbels' propaganda during the war; it not only helped to prevent a coherent German resistance movement to Nazism emerging, even during the final days of the Third Reich, but also represented the ideological basis of collaborationism with fascism in much of Europe. It would be wrong to suggest that it was only fascists who collaborated with the Nazis, however, for careerists, opportunists, pacifists and those who desired peace with Germany also seized the opportunities created by the collapse of resistance to Nazism in Austria, Czechoslovakia, Poland, Denmark, Norway, The Netherlands, Belgium and France between 1938 and 1940. It would also be misleading to suggest that all fascists were pro-Hitler or that they welcomed German domination. Although many western European fascists were in favour of appeasement during the 1930s, and at no stage did Sir Oswald Mosley of the British Union of Fascists or Léon Degrelle of the Belgian Rexist Party ever criticise any of Hitler's actions, for example, there was always tension between the national interests of different European states.

Hitler was well aware that German interests were often fundamentally opposed to the revisionist claims of other countries' nationalist proponents, as can be seen in the conflicting German and French nationalists' claims to Alsace-Lorraine. At the core of fascism was an extreme form of nationalism and Hitler was realistic enough to see that the fascists of other countries were often opposed to the claims of German nationalism. This was why Hitler, unlike Mussolini, was so reluctant to subsidise other manifestations of fascism. Only where short-term, tactical gains could be achieved, as with his funding of fascist 'fifth columns' in Austria and the Sudetenland in 1938 and in his encouragement of defeatist feelings in western Europe in 1940, did Hitler give any thought to aiding foreign fascist movements. Similarly, his wooing of Mussolini in 1936 caused Hitler temporarily to relinquish German claims to the German-speaking Alto Adige region of Italy.

At the core of the Nazi ideals behind the creation of the 'new order' was an unresolved tension between German national interests and the Nazi creation of a new Europe (*europäische Neuordnung*). If the German hegemony of Europe was to be maintained by consent rather than force after the rapid success of the *Blitzkrieg* in northern and western Europe between March and June 1940, it was necessary for some form of collaboration with the defeated nations. While there was no precedent for this and the very speed of events meant that ad hoc solutions to the problems created by the rapid German victories were necessary, Nazi priorities did not alter. In the 'new order', the defeated western nations would be in a relatively privileged position, for while a variety of different forms of settlement was forced on the defeated nations by Hitler, there was a marked contrast between his treatment of western and eastern European nations during the war.

Perhaps a more accurate indicator of Nazi plans for the 'new order' was provided by the treatment of European forced labourers in Germany during the war. By 1944, over 7 million foreign labourers in Germany were providing the necessary manpower to prevent the collapse of the war economy. Although the prospect of Germany's imminent defeat had reduced the living standards for all forced-labour groups of people by that stage, western European labourers (with the exception of the Italian 'traitors', as the Nazis regarded them after Italy's surrender to the Allies in 1943) were much better treated than any others.

Hitler's post-conquest policies

Although Nazi terms in the armistices made with the defeated nations were often harsh, the treatment of most conquered peoples was relatively civilised when compared with events following the invasion of Poland in 1939 and the barbarities inflicted during Operation Barbarossa after June 1941. In Denmark, the political structure of the state remained unaltered. In Norway, Vidkun Quisling, the fascist leader of the *Nasjonal Samling* (National Unification) Party, conducted a *coup d'état* in 1940 but was usually ignored by Hitler, who preferred to use a council of state or direct military rule with which to govern Norway. Similarly, after the German invasion of their countries, Anton Mussert in The Netherlands and Léon Degrelle in Belgium were given no effective power and acted only as 'cheerleaders' for the Nazis. The same was true of the Hungarian fascist leader, Ferenc Szálasi, who had no real independence of action after the German invasion of his country in 1944 and who diligently implemented Nazi policies when he became head of a puppet government for a short period at the beginning of 1945.

In spite of the rapid collapse of many European countries' resistance to Hitler in 1940 and the scapegoat role that many native fascists were accorded in anti-fascist propaganda, there is little evidence that a 'fifth column' existed in any country or that the conquered nations' speedy defeat can be explained as resulting from internal sabotage or the work of enemy agents. In France, the native fascists' opposition to the Second World War was not the cause of France's defeat and neither did the inclusion of fascist ideas in French intellectual discourse during the 1930s prove the undoing of the French Third Republic.

Hitler's treatment of France

The German armistice with France of 22 June 1940, which was signed in the same railway carriage at Compiègne which had been used for the signing of the armistice with Germany at the end of the First World War, imposed massive reparations, forcing France to meet the costs of the German occupation of the country. It also transferred Alsace and Lorraine to Germany once more and made 1½ million French prisoners of war hostages. The terms of the armistice divided France into three separate areas: the 'forbidden zone' of the Pas de Calais; the occupied zone of the north and west, which was under direct military rule; and the unoccupied or 'free zone' of central and southern France, where the Vichy regime, under the leadership of Marshal Henri Pétain, was based. The final peace treaty was postponed until the end of the war, but the Nazis envisaged the 'ethnic cleansing' and Germanisation of the region of Burgundy.

In fact, Hitler paid little attention to the terms of the armistice, large numbers of Jewish and French people being forcibly ejected from Alsace and Lorraine and dumped in the 'free zone', contrary to the spirit of the armistice, for example. The Vichy regime (which took its name from the spa town where Pétain's collaborationist regime was centred from June 1940) proved to be authoritarian and right wing, with fascist trappings. Although its Catholic ethos makes it doubtful whether the term 'fascist' can accurately be applied to the Vichy regime, it was certainly both anti-Semitic and anti-communist, two central characteristics of fascist regimes (these characteristics made it similar to the dictatorships of Miklós Horthy in Hungary and King Carol II in Romania). The authoritarian nature of the Vichy regime can be seen in the fact that the two leading French neo-fascist collaborationists, Marcel Déat and Jacques Doriot, were forbidden to operate in Vichy until the Nazis decreed otherwise. Only in 1942, when the war swung decisively against Hitler, did the façade of French sovereignty in Vichy give way as the Nazis entered the unoccupied zone to form a second front as a defensive precaution against a potential Allied invasion from the south.

Fascist fellow travellers

If the fascists of other countries were not given power or actively encouraged by Hitler, except for reasons of potential fifth-column manipulation (which played little role in actual events), circumstances nevertheless decreed that they became more significant than Hitler had intended. Although collaboration with the Nazis was a much wider phenomenon than that of fascist fellow travellers who openly supported the Nazis, there can be little doubt that many western European movements, such as the Belgian Rexist Party, actively participated in the Nazi administration of occupied Europe, including criminal activities. Some provided brigades for the *Waffen-SS* (armed SS) divisions that were involved in Operation

Barbarossa on the Eastern Front and some were implicated in massacres of Jews and civilians. Other fascists, most notoriously in France and Belgium, joined the Nazi security forces that were involved in fighting resistance movements, while the international Charlemagne Division of the SS defended the remnants of the Third Reich in a last stand in Berlin in 1945.

The achievement of Hitler's long-term aims was put on hold during the war and it is unclear what the future would have held for a Nazi-dominated Europe. One of the motives of those who collaborated with the Nazis was undoubtedly the alleged benefits with which they thought their co-operation would be rewarded when the Nazi 'new order' was finally implemented (this was certainly the basis for Pierre Laval's collaborationist policy when he was prime minister of the Vichy regime between 1942 and 1944). The fact that Hitler was not interested in paying Franco's price (a North African empire) for Spain's entrance into the Second World War suggests that despite the relatively civilised treatment meted out to western European nations Hitler's vision of the 'new order' was a German-dominated Europe, not a European 'community of nations'. The Nazis' looting of French national treasures and Göring's (Hitler's deputy) plundering of stolen art collections were furthermore indicative of the Nazis' rapacious greed, even in their dealings with those whom they did not deem 'racially inferior'. Massive requisitioning of industrial equipment, minerals, factories and foodstuffs, in addition to the demand for financial reparations, were all typical of the Nazis' claims on defeated nations. As the *Blitzkrieg* in the Soviet Union ground to a halt from 1943, so 'total war' necessitated the provision of forced labour by the defeated nations in order to service Germany's war on two fronts.

Racial war

If hostilities in western Europe during the Second World War bore some relation to the accepted conventions of warfare, the same could not be said for those on the Eastern Front. It was here that the horrific consequences of the Nazi rejection of human compassion and egalitarianism in its pursuit of national 'rebirth' became manifest and that the worst atrocities were committed in order to rid the world of 'decadence'. The war in the east was regarded by the Nazis from the outset as an exterminatory war which would destroy the Slavic 'Asiatic hordes', the 'bastardised Jewish race' and the 'Jewish bacillus' of communism. These aims were inherent from the beginning of the war, but as the conditions of warfare turned from a *Blitzkrieg* into a static war so the 'industrial killing' of 'racial enemies' was given the highest priority. Conditions in Poland worsened progressively from 1939 to 1944, with the extermination of the Polish intelligentsia, the ghettoisation and systematic murder of Jewish people following the introduction of the death camps at Chelmno, Majdanek, Belzec, Sobibor, Treblinka and Auschwitz, which decimated Polish Jewry years before Auschwitz became the centre for the mass murder of European Jews. (The generally accepted estimate given for the number of Jewish people who died in the Holocaust is 6 million, mainly at death camps like Auschwitz and Treblinka.)

Children peer from behind barbed wire as they await their release during the liberation of the Auschwitz concentration camp, January 1945.

The Nazis' attempted genocide of European Jewry makes the Holocaust a horrifyingly unique phenomenon, but other groups of people were also ferociously persecuted and destroyed, among them the Sinti and Roma communities of Gypsies, homosexuals, communists, socialists and mentally and physically disabled people. Like Jewish people, they were either shot, given lethal injections or slowly worked to death, existing on food rations that were calculated to ensure that they wasted away agonisingly. The 'euthanasia' programme that was carried out in German institutions was a gruesome prototype of the 'industrial-production' process of mass killing that was later perfected at Auschwitz, and the Nazis congratulated themselves on having replaced the 'messy' killings of Jews by SS *Einsatzgruppen* following the invasion of Poland and Russia with more 'modern' methods of extermination. In fact, in terms of the number of people who died, the 'cull' of non-Jewish people in the east dwarfs even that of the Jews, with between 10 and 20 million Poles, Russians, people of other Soviet nationalities and southern Europeans being murdered.

The war in the east

What made Operation Barbarossa, the German invasion of the Soviet Union which began in June 1941, truly horrific were the Nazi-determined rules of engagement and the Nazis' actual practice of warfare. Hitler attacked the Soviet

Union without making any declaration of war and the *Wehrmacht* disregarded the Geneva Conventions from the outset. All captured Soviet political commissars (heads of government departments) were shot, while captured prisoners of war were left to starve to death. The SS *Einsatzgruppen* 'mopped up' behind the lines, murdering not only communists but also systematically killing all the Jews that they could find, usually by means of mass shooting. The shortage of qualified, elite, SS 'Aryan' murderers meant that such activities were often subcontracted to others, including the security forces of collaborationist fascist and nationalist minorities in the Soviet Union; the *Wehrmacht*, too, became heavily implicated in the massacres of civilians, prisoners of war and Jews. The extension of such terrible practices to incorporate the attempted extermination of European Jewry and the destruction of other 'undesirable' minorities led to 'ordinary' police reservists and medical staff being asked to volunteer for such 'special duties' (although no penalties were taken against those who refused to become involved).

The carnage of the Eastern Front represented the manifestation of both an ideological and political conflict and 'racial war', and also reflected the fact that the *Blitzkrieg* strategy was inappropriate for hostilities against the Soviet Union. Although Stalin had considerably weakened his military strength by ordering the massacre of the officer corps of the Red army during the Great Purges of 1937 to 1938, the Soviet Union's difficult geographical terrain and hostile climate, Stalin's ability to transfer seemingly inexhaustible numbers of fresh troops from the Far East to the Soviet Union, as well as the superiority of some Soviet military equipment, negated the element of surprise in Hitler's attack and denied Germany an easy victory. While the German assault made deep inroads into the Soviet Union (with massive losses for the Germans, as well as over 2 million Soviet casualties), the offensive ground to a halt before Moscow, Leningrad (Saint Petersburg) and Stalingrad (Volgograd) in the winter of 1941. The ensuing stalemate lasted for a year before the Soviet forces successfully broke out in 1943 and turned the war around by waging Red army *Blitzkrieg*, forcing an eventual German retreat, despite Hitler's refusal to sanction a withdrawal. For the German soldiers, the war in the east came to resemble the static warfare of the First World War.

Hitler's vision for the east

While the preparatory phases of 'ethnic cleansing' – death and destruction – were the only aspects of the 'new order' to be implemented, the Nazi project for the Jewish people's 'resettlement in the east' (that is, before the term became a euphemism for the Holocaust) included various grandiose plans for the 'Germanic' future. Nazi medical and social-welfare programmes envisaged the 'racial health' of the community rather than the individual as being the basis of their policies. Achieving communal 'racial health' meant positive discrimination in favour of, and state assistance for, the 'fit' and varying degrees of negative discrimination against the 'unfit', from prejudice, ostracism, segregation, incarceration, to 'resettlement' and finally death. If *Hitler's table talk*[3] is to be believed (and it is unclear how much his ramblings during the latter stages of the war were the products of his progressive inability to grasp practical realities), he envisioned a Jewish-free, de-urbanised Europe, with German settlers acting as the feudal overlords of any surviving, enslaved Slavs on vast eastern estates. Other Nazis had more 'practical' visions: Albert Speer, Hitler's official architect, for example, drew up plans for gigantic monuments so that future generations could appreciate the achievements of the Nazi state. Although there was no formal Nazi blueprint for the 'new order', there was no shortage of plans for it, even in the chaotic conditions of war. The Nazi Colonial Office envisaged a Nazi-controlled Europe which employed vassal populations and colonial conquests in Africa as the source of Germany's food and raw materials. For their part, Nazi statisticians and population planners envisaged the forced transfer of 30 million Slavs to western Siberia in order to make way for Germans to 'modernise' eastern Europe.

The reality behind such Nazi visions was world war, death and destruction, resulting in the attempted genocide of European Jewry, the indiscriminate slaughter of the Slavic populations of Europe and the premature deaths of millions of Germans, Americans and western Europeans. By the end of the Second World War much of Europe had been reduced to rubble and the continent would be politically and geographically divided for the following 50 years. All this horror resulted from the mythical and pseudo-scientific pretensions of the Nazi state and its attempt to create the fascist 'new order' in its most radical, racist form.

Document case study

The fascist 'new order'

7.1 A contemporary French view of the fascist 'new man'

A certain way of thinking characteristic of the late nineteenth and early twentieth century had provided European humanity with the basis of a renaissance such as it had not seen for centuries, for a revolution as total as that of an hour hand returning to the same point on the clock face . . . The new man has appeared in uncompromised fullness in Italy and Germany . . . The Hitlerian has been formed from the convergence of these elements: the fighter of the Great War moulded in the *Sturmtruppen* or airforce, and who turned into the fanatic of the *Freikorps*, the terrorist assassin who killed Rathenau; the boy scout, the *Wandervogel* trekking from youth hostel to youth hostel from one end of Europe to the other in search of an ill-defined salvation; the communist hit man; the neurasthenic inspired by the example of the Italian Fascists as well as the American gangsters, the mercenaries of the Chinese wars, the soldiers of the Foreign Legion.

Source: Pierre Drieu la Rochelle, *Renaissance de l'homme européen*, Paris, 1941, translated by Roger Griffin, in R. Griffin (ed.), *Fascism: a reader*, Oxford, 1995, pp. 202–3

7.2 A contemporary Nazi scientist's view

2 Ethnic Settlement

1) The *Raum* [space] to be won shall exclusively serve German people and the German future; German blood has been spilled for this goal only. The newly acquired land must be made empty of all foreign ethnic elements; all foreign races, foreign people are to be resettled.

2) The retention of foreign peoples and inhabitants of lesser racial value will inevitably result in a bastardisation of German settlers, which must lead to a consequential weakening of the strength of the German *Volk* [people] and their cultural capabilities. The German people in the East shall not be merely a linguistically 'Germanised' hybrid population, but true and pure German people. We do not need a bastard population there with Polish characteristics and Polish cultural incapability which is determined by blood! All the great peoples of pre-history have been brought to ruin by such hybridisation.

Source: memorandum from Professor Otto Reche (Leipzig) to Professor Albert Brachmann (Königsberg), quoted in M. Burleigh, *Germany turns eastwards*, Cambridge, 1988, p. 168

7.3 Nazi plans for the implementation of the 'Final Solution'

Under appropriate direction the Jews are to be utilised for work in the East in an expedient manner in the course of the Final Solution. In large [labour] columns, with the sexes separated, Jews capable of work will be moved into these areas as they build roads, during which a large proportion will no doubt drop out through natural reduction. The remnant that eventually remains will require suitable treatment; because it will without doubt represent the most physically resistant part, it consists of a natural selection that could, on its release, become the germ cell of a new Jewish revival. Europe is to be combed through from West to East in the course of the practical implementation of the Final Solution.

Source: *Obergruppenführer* Reinhard Heydrich, chief of the SS *Sicherheitsdienst* (SD), the security police, to the Wannsee Conference, 20 January 1942

Document case-study questions

1 What does 7.1 tell us about the main characteristics of the Nazi 'new man'?

2 What does 7.2 suggest about the plans for ethnic cleansing in Poland?

3 What does 7.3 imply about the development of the 'Final Solution' of the 'Jewish question'?

4 What do the sources suggest about the projected nature of the Nazi 'new order'?

Notes and references

1 *Hitler's secret book*, New York, 1961.

2 R. Overy, *The Nazi economic recovery, 1932–38*, London, 1982.

3 H. R. Trevor-Roper (ed.), *Hitler's table talk, 1941–44*, London, 1953.

8 The end of fascism?

The defeat of Nazism in 1945 brought the era of fascism to an end. The only point of agreement between the members of the 'grand alliance' between Britain, the United States and the Soviet Union that had been formed to defeat Hitler after 1941 was that the war should not be concluded until the 'unconditional surrender' of Germany (and Japan) had been achieved. Once this had been accomplished, an attempt was made to obliterate the memory of fascism in much of Europe. Fascism was banned in Italy and in Germany the Allies moved rapidly to 're-educate' the population. They established what later became the communist state of East Germany (*Deutsche Demokratische Republik*, DDR), also known as the German Democratic Republic (GDR), in the Soviet zone of occupation and merged the three western, 'de-Nazified' zones, initially controlled by Britain, the United States and France, into the Federal Republic of Germany (*Bundesrepublik Deutschland*, BRD), or West Germany. There was a settling of scores in all European states, with up to 10,000 summary executions occurring in Italy, perhaps 20,000 in France and death sentences being passed on notorious collaborators in most European nations. The Nuremberg Trials of 1946, in which justice was meted out to the surviving Nazi leaders, imposed not only immediate death sentences or incarceration upon them but also appeared to confirm the collective will to wipe out fascism for ever.

The purge of former Nazis and fascists rapidly declined in ferocity on both sides of the 'Iron Curtain', the ideological divide which polarised Europe during the Cold War era. As the former wartime Allies fell out with each other, former fascists were conveniently accorded new, Cold War-warrior roles. Following a different political agenda, former fascists and a new generation of fascists began developing fresh ideas which incorporated both old fascist myths and contemporary pragmatic realities. In Italy, Germany, France and elsewhere, proponents of new forms of ultra-nationalism, federal 'Euro-fascism' and racial populism emerged to criticise the political establishment. While anti-Semitism declined in intensity, immigrants to Europe and their descendants, particularly those originally from Third World countries, were singled out by racists to play the role of scapegoats for their countries' economic and social malaise. Fascism may have retreated to the margins of European politics, but ultra-nationalistic and anti-immigrant voices advocating 'ethnic cleansing' emerged as a significant political subculture in much of Europe. This subculture, which also manifested itself in the former Soviet Union and its satellite countries after the collapse of European communism between 1989 and 1991, appeared to have marked affinities with inter-war fascism.

The unconditional surrender of Germany

The reduction of much of Germany to rubble in 1945 signified not only the crushing of the Axis powers but also the end of the European dominance of world affairs. The vast material and human resources of the United States and the Soviet Union had won the war for the 'united nations' of the 'grand alliance' and it was these superpowers which would control the rebuilding of the new order. Yet the wartime alliance of the United States and the Soviet Union rapidly disintegrated and Europe was split by the ideological divisions between the 'liberal/capitalist/US' West and the 'socialist/Soviet' East.

In most European states, memories of fascism and Nazism faded rapidly in the immediate aftermath of the war, and after the onset of the Cold War in the late 1940s former fascists were able to re-establish themselves in civilian life on both sides of the Iron Curtain. In the Soviet Union especially, the ethnic tensions which had been inflamed during the Nazi era were not resolved but merely suppressed, while in many countries in western Europe small groups of fascists attempted to whip up, organise and politicise racial tensions. Despite the relegation of Nazism's ideological legacy to the status of a political underground movement, fascism would become a deep-rooted and disturbing undercurrent within future European developments.

The legacy of Nazism

The immediate aftermath of the Second World War suggested that fascism was a spent force in European politics. Both Hitler and Mussolini had met inglorious ends. The 'invincible' *Führer* committed suicide in his Berlin bunker on 30 April 1945, after which his followers doused his body in petrol and burnt it in what could be regarded as a grotesque parody of the funeral pyre which his Wagnerian imagination might have dreamed up. Two days earlier, the 'infallible' *Duce* had been shot dead by Italian partisans and his body was then strung up upside down, alongside that of his mistress, from a Milanese petrol station; it was perhaps a fitting end for a leader who had transformed politics into a theatrical spectacle.

The summary justice that was immediately meted out to all those who were believed to have collaborated with the Nazis or Fascists led to a significant purge of fascist sympathisers, particularly in those areas that were occupied by the Soviet Red Army and secret police (NKVD), as well as in France, where there were more executions than in either the western occupied zones of Germany or Italy in the aftermath of the war. Having suffered so many deaths (up to 30 million people died as a direct result of the war in Europe) and so much destruction, it was not surprising that the Nazis and their collaborators should have been held responsible for bringing about the most destructive war in Europe's history. The almost daily revelation in 1945 of the Nazi atrocities that had been carried out during the war – symbolised by the images of the emaciated corpses of concentration-camp victims being bulldozed into mass graves – created a climate of public revulsion in which the desire permanently to destroy fascist ideas and influences was evident.

Nazism: the issue of responsibility

It was in this atmosphere that the Nuremberg Trials were planned in 1946. They were intended to be a final public settling of scores with the surviving Nazi leaders and were designed to demonstrate unequivocally the criminality of the Nazi regime and the corresponding need for a just retribution to be made before a final line could be drawn under the Second World War and Europe could begin the task of rebuilding its future. Although the Nuremberg Trials proved the personal responsibility of the Nazi leaders for the atrocities that had been systematically committed by the Nazi regime, they also revealed the divisions that were developing between the Allies and furthermore raised disturbing questions as to the moral implications of the Allied wartime strategy of the saturation-bombing of German cities, such as Hamburg and Dresden. They also led many people to ask whether some of the activities of the SS and the Gestapo were worse than those of the Soviet NKVD in those parts of Europe that it occupied following their liberation from the Nazis. (Indeed, it later came to light that the NKVD had been responsible for the Katyn massacre, in which agents of the Soviet secret police had slaughtered many members of the Polish officer corps.)

Some Nazi leaders committed suicide, most notably Göring, who followed the precedent set by Hitler, Goebbels and Himmler. Others, like Wilhelm Frick, Joachim von Ribbentrop and Alfred Rosenberg, were either hanged or, like Albert Speer and Rudolf Hess, incarcerated in Spandau prison in Berlin. If they had survived the immediate aftermath of the war, however, many of the lesser functionaries of the fascist regimes stood a good chance of avoiding retribution entirely, for the Cold War rivalry of the two superpowers placed a high premium on their technological or military skills, particularly in the Soviet bloc. As a result of the polarisation of the Cold War, communists rather than fascists came to be regarded as the new 'fifth column' in western Europe.

A changing political agenda

After the initial retributions had been carried out, those on both sides of the Iron Curtain tried to draw a line beneath the Second World War. Former fascists and nationalists were recruited by the American Central Intelligence Agency (CIA) to undertake anti-communist activities during the Cold War period in Albania and the Soviet Union (usually with disastrous consequences, because their operations were often compromised by Kim Philby, the Soviet spy working in MI6, the British government's intelligence agency). Both the USA and the Soviet Union competed for German scientists to work in the arms and space races. While the search for those Nazis who were responsible for the massacres of Jews, the implementation of the Holocaust and the murder of people from other ethnic minorities continued, only Jewish communities regarded it as a top priority in the changed political agenda of Cold War Europe.

Although the extermination of militant forms of fascism rapidly became a decreased political priority during the Cold War and many former fascists and Nazis rose to responsible positions on both sides of the Iron Curtain, ideological fascists had little influence anywhere in Europe. Because West Germany became the principal beneficiary of American investment in Europe following the implementation of the Marshall Plan, which was designed to aid European revival, in 1948, any attempts to revive fascism had little impact there. The banning of Nazism in Germany and Fascism in Italy can be said to have been unnecessary, for it was only when economic difficulties arose or domestic communist parties posed a temporary political threat that any interest was shown in reviving fascism in any European country, and then always in a diluted or covert form.

Fascism in post-war Italy and Germany

Following the Cold War change in political priorities, those former fascists who had survived retribution slowly re-emerged. The first example of this, and the most important, was in Italy, where as early as 1945 former Fascists infiltrated the Party of the Common Man (*Uomo Qualungue*, UQ), which won 20 per cent of the popular vote in Rome and Naples. In December 1946, radical Fascist survivors of the Italian Social Republic formed the Italian Social Movement (*Movimento Sociale Italiano*, MSI) which won 2 per cent of the popular vote in the 1948 election, giving it six seats in the Chamber of Deputies. Although it rapidly became divided between radical, neo-fascist and anti-communist, conservative factions, the MSI remained the most significant post-war link with the Fascist tradition until it was replaced by the *Alleanza Nazionale* (AN) in 1994. The Fascist continuity within the MSI was symbolised by the election to its leadership of Giorgio Almirante, a junior functionary in the Italian Social Republic, and by the MSI's flag, an Italian tricolour in the shape of a flame flickering above a funeral bier (for the initiated, it betokened the spirit of Mussolini rising from his ashes).

In the western zones of Germany a similar pattern emerged. (It should be noted, however, that no German political party was allowed to call itself 'national socialist', while denying that the Holocaust had happened was a criminal offence in the Federal Republic, which also paid out considerable compensation to the state of Israel for the Nazis' murder of millions of Jewish people.) The right-wing, nationalist German Conservative Party-German Right Party (DKP-DRP), founded in 1946, attracted many former Nazis. Although it was swiftly banned under the new Basic Law of the Federal Republic, the rump of the DKP-DRP merged with smaller groups to form the Socialist Reich Party (SRP) in 1949, which, although significant in the early 1950s, rapidly faded after 1953. It was not until 1964 that former Nazis were again attracted to a political party, this time the extreme-nationalistic National Democratic Party (NDP) under Adolf von Thadden; it also gained significant support in the traditionally sympathetic rural Protestant areas. The NDP remained the most significant voice on the far right until the 1980s.

American investment in, and military support of, Germany, in particular through the Marshall Plan and the North Atlantic Treaty Organisation (NATO), provided an essential antidote to the threat posed by communism and the Soviet

Union and created the necessary conditions for the economic growth and political stability which buttressed democracy in western Europe. Fascism therefore failed to gain the political space in which the movement could re-emerge in any significant form.

Crypto-fascism in southern Europe

Despite the political turbulence of 1968 and the constant undercurrent of both right- and left-wing terrorism during the 1970s, the post-war period generally enjoyed the conditions necessary for the smooth functioning of democracy in much of western and northern Europe, although there were significant exceptions. The survivors of the fascist era, the Salazar and Franco regimes in Portugal and Spain respectively, both continued into the 1970s. Neither Salazar nor Franco were authentic fascists and both became increasingly keen anti-communists after 1945, simultaneously, however, distancing themselves as far as possible from the legacy of fascism while still maintaining their hostility to liberalism and democracy. Similarly, the military regime of the 'Colonels' in Greece between 1967 and 1974 also practised a militant form of anti-communism while at the same time persecuting liberals and denouncing American 'decadence' (a policy which, although transparently contradictory, did not lead to outside intervention). All three regimes were cold-shouldered by their erstwhile allies – those countries that now belonged to NATO – and remained in diplomatic isolation.

Other manifestations of neo-fascism

Elsewhere in Europe, authentic or nostalgic fascist movements were perceived as political eccentricities, odd throwbacks to a bygone age. Some extremists or racists tried to resurrect the Nazi tradition by advocating a virulent form of anti-Semitism and fomenting political violence. Others, particularly in Italy, borrowed the tactics of the communist terrorist group the Red Brigade, and a small neo-fascist cell was responsible for the outrage at Bologna's railway station in 1980 in which 85 people died. In Britain, Sir Oswald Mosley, who, by 1947, was concerned with the prospect of Europe being overrun by the 'Asiatic hordes' and becoming subject to Soviet domination, identified what he perceived to be the need to rally the 'decadent' West and strive for the creation of the 'Thought-Deed' man (a heroic man of action who would defend European culture and civilisation from liberal decadence and communism), representing a new stage of evolution which would go 'beyond fascism and democracy'. But Mosley's Europeanism and gloomy prognostications fell on deaf ears and he remained on the fringes of political life, with his new Union Movement, which he founded in 1948, having only a negligible impact on Britain. Indeed, more blatant imitations of the Fascist and Nazi past, as well as attempts to deny the reality of the attempted genocide of European Jewry, made even less impact, although they received more publicity.

'Euro-fascism'

The most sustained and influential attempts to revive the fascist tradition were achieved by more subtle means. The failure of both national neo-fascist and 'Euro-fascist' movements to get off the ground after neo-fascist conferences held at Malmö (1951) and Venice (1962) led to the more intelligent of the former fascists and the new generation of intellectual neo-fascists to attempt to infiltrate and permeate orthodox political and parliamentary cultures. Right-wing parties throughout Europe in particular became the targets of the neo-fascist attempts to influence mainstream politics and political ideas. Neo-fascist revisionist attempts to package fascist ideas in new ways through the use of coded language or by presenting extreme-right-wing or nationalistic sentiments as deriving from more acceptable origins than Fascism or Nazism tried to whitewash their historical fascist inheritance.

Some of the more sophisticated neo-fascists today thus promote ideas of national 'rebirth' drawn from 'Strasserite' (named after the Nazi ideologist Gregor Strasser) ideas or a 'third position', a form of national socialism which seeks a path which is neither capitalist or communist (and even expresses solidarity with Muammar Ghaddafi's regime in Libya and the Palestinians, both of which may be perceived as being oppressed by the USA and Israel). Alternatively, they base their ideas on the concept of a 'conservative revolution' put forward by radical elitists like the Italian and German 'conservative revolutionaries' Julius Evola and Ernst Jünger, who were either peripheral to Fascism and Nazism or actually rejected them. In addition, an intellectual, neo-fascist, 'new right' has emerged, influenced by Alain de Benoist, whose intellectual origins lie in France but which has had a major impact, not just on Jean-Marie Le Pen's anti-immigration party, the *Front National* (FN), but also on the far-right political culture of many countries, especially Germany and Italy.

Such attempts to adapt the political discourse on racial intolerance to an era in which liberal civilisation, in stark contrast to the inter-war period, has no longer been felt to have been in crisis has not created a credible threat to liberalism. In fact, fascism, both as an electoral and a paramilitary force, seems destined to remain highly marginalised as long as the existing socio-economic conditions of relative stability prevail. Nevertheless, the neo-fascist 'new right's' celebration of cultural differences has provided intellectual fascists with many effective euphemisms with which to attack liberalism, multi-culturalism and universal human rights.

The 'Holocaust denial'

Another important current of intellectual fascism has focused on playing down the horrors of the Third Reich which, in its crudest form, means flatly denying that the mass extermination of Jews ever happened (a viewpoint called the 'Holocaust denial'). A more subtle tactic that is used is 'revising' the historical record, for example, by portraying the Nazi regime as a victim of British or Soviet ill-treatment (but conveniently omitting any mention of Hitler's aggressive foreign-policy acts which provoked the Second World War in the first place). Another favoured tactic is indulging in so-called 'relativism', which suggests that 'atrocities' committed by the Allies, like the bombing of Dresden or Hiroshima, were as bad as, if not worse than, those perpetrated in the Nazi death camps.

The new racism

In general terms, it may safely be assumed that the revolutionary potential of fascism was destroyed in 1945. Certainly, the efforts of the militant, electoral and intellectual fascists to undermine the political framework of Europe have failed. After the Soviet Union began to collapse in the late 1980s it was clear that the democratic politics of the Western tradition had broadly prevailed, though with sharply varying degrees of stability, prosperity and respect for human rights. Yet fascism, and in particular Nazism, had left a disturbing legacy in one important area. The resentment of mass immigration in parts of Europe, the widespread nostalgia for a pure 'cultural identity' and the readiness to resort to 'ethnic cleansing' in the former Yugoslavia during the 1990s perpetuated some of the most dangerous fascist fantasies about a racially and culturally homogeneous 'national community' and displayed both a direct imitation of, and linkage to, some of the more dangerous and intellectually spurious aspects of Nazism. Racism and extreme nationalism have not disappeared – as long as the fabric of society is not torn apart by socio-economic tensions they just remain dormant.

Racial populism

Although the collapse of communism in the Soviet Union and eastern Europe between 1989 and 1991 removed one of the main fears which had fed support for fascism in the inter-war period, the 1990s saw an increase in ethnic tensions in parts of the European continent and the rise of a form of racial populism (often referred to as racism or xenophobia) which reminded many political commentators of the background to Hitler's seizure of power. Not only did anti-Semitism remain an enduring political undercurrent but there were also two new developments that increased ethnic tension. Firstly, the political and economic success of the European Economic Community (EEC), now called the European Union (EU), encouraged immigration from Third World countries to some member states. This sometimes led to xenophobia, especially in those regions where there had been earlier waves of immigration. For example, 'black' (coloured) people had immigrated from Commonwealth countries to Britain and Algerians to France, while there had also been a large influx of *Gastarbeiter* ('guest-workers') and asylum-seekers into both West and East Germany, Switzerland and Austria. Secondly, such waves of immigration had encouraged the growth of anti-immigration movements in both Britain and France from the 1960s, a trend which was to spread to other EEC countries from the 1970s. One symptom of this development was the emergence of racial-populist movements in Britain and France which had clear links to the fascist past.

Anti-immigrant movements in western Europe

It should be stressed that neither the National Front (formed in 1966) nor the British National Party (formed in 1983) in Britain regard themselves as fascist, but nevertheless both have demonstrable connections in terms of their membership and ideology with pre- and post-war fascism, the British fascist tradition (Mosley's movement and Arthur Leese's inter-war racially nationalist Imperial Fascist League), as well as Nazism. Having peaked in the late 1970s, by the late 1990s electoral fascism in Britain had faded into insignificance, but in France the *Front National*, under Le Pen, has used its policy of anti-immigration so effectively that it has established itself as a 'third force' in French politics. Although single-issue movements are usually limited in their potential and staying power, Le Pen eschewed the radicalism of a fascist revolutionary programme and focused instead on blaming immigrants for the continuing high unemployment levels in France, which have recently been exacerbated by both the social costs of the EU and the need to meet the strict convergence criteria imposed before 1999 by the creation of a single European currency.

Since 1991, the costs of German re-unification (particularly with regard to the social and modernisation problems of the former East Germany), together with the need to meet the budgetary convergence criteria of the single European currency, have also led to record unemployment levels in Germany. *Gastarbeiter* have become the scapegoats for these economic and social difficulties, with racist and political violence increasingly being aimed primarily at non-EU immigrants, particularly from Turkey, and anti-immigrant, nationalist movements, such as the Republican Party (*Die Republikaner*, REP), having grown in membership.

In Italy, the growth of a powerful regional movement in the north, the *Lega Nord* (Northern League), and the success of the reformed neo-Fascist MSI, the AN, in becoming the coalition partner of Silvio Berlusconi's *Forza Italia*, has resulted in tight restrictions being imposed on the influx of political refugees and immigrants from the former Yugoslavia and Albania into Italy. However, no party has yet played the racist card in respect of the country's growing population (currently over 1.5 million) of immigrants from North Africa. In Austria, Jürgen Haider's Austrian Freedom Party (*Freiheitliche Partei Österreichs*) has also established a sizcable electoral base by having come to be regarded as the 'protector' of national identity and pride.

Fascism and ethnicity in eastern Europe

Parties and movements that play on fears of a loss of cultural identity have proliferated in the former Soviet Union, most strikingly in Russia. At one point, the leader of the perversely named Liberal Democratic Party of Russia (LDPR), Vladimir Zhirinovsky, was confidently holding out the prospect of a purge of 'foreign' peoples in Russia, an alliance with a reconstituted Third Reich and giving military aid to the USA to help it to deal with its ethnic problems.

Zhirinovsky even gained 23 per cent of the popular vote in Russia's parliamentary elections of December 1993, when the chaos of the post-Soviet era was at its height, but his popularity subsequently waned rapidly as stability temporarily returned.

Movements such as the French FN, the German REPS, the Italian AN and the Russian LDPR skilfully combine faint echoes of inter-war fascism with the necessary pragmatic readjustments to enable them to adapt their message to the stable conditions of post-war Europe, as well as to the very different problems (particularly immigration) that have been experienced. In one part of Europe, however, the events that occurred after the collapse of the Soviet Union displayed to a greater degree the disturbing social and psychological energies that had fuelled Nazism. The collapse of the former Yugoslavia and the resulting struggle for Bosnia between 1991 and 1995 not only led to the horrors of 'ethnic cleansing' but also to a reactivation of the deep-rooted historical tensions between the Serb, Croat and Moslem populations. These tensions had, until then, most recently been fanned during the Second World War, when the Croatian *Ustasha* ('Insurgent') movement, in collaboration with the Nazis, was responsible for the murder of at least 500,000 Serbs and was also implicated in the Holocaust of the Jewish population.

The future of fascism

Despite the existence of some isolated pockets of ethnic tension and organised racism, the future of fascism is far from rosy. There will always be a minute percentage of extreme nationalists who are attracted to, rather than repelled by, the achievements of Mussolini or Hitler, however, and there may well be flashpoints of ethnic tension in the future which summon forth political ideas and actions that are reminiscent of fascism. Moreover, the marked contrast between the success of the European Union and the difficulties experienced by the former communist countries in adjusting to the free-market economy may also give rise to conditions in which fascism could take root. There are furthermore significant tensions between those who envisage a fully integrated Europe and those who want a much looser confederation which will not threaten national sovereignties and identities. Such rifts create the political space in which extremist forms of ultra-nationalism may develop.

It needs to be stressed, however, that most nationalist movements are both constitutional and law-abiding in their behaviour and that the prospect of the resurgence of a truly fascist – that is, revolutionary – form of nationalist politics is remote, even in those countries whose transition to Western-style democracy and politics is causing acute social tensions. The facts that ethnic minorities have been singled out as scapegoats for domestic problems, that political thugs in the heart of Europe have been responsible for atrocities against immigrants and that modern economics maintains high levels of structural unemployment suggest that the 'deadly trunk of fascism', in Primo Levi's words, will continue to grow new shoots.

However, the Second World War revealed the nightmare scenario which lurks behind the fascist dream of a rejuvenated national community. Indeed, it could be said that the true threat to humanity is not likely to come from revolutionary nationalism but from other, even more destructive, sources, such as a modern economic system that is blind to the necessity of protecting the ecosystem in order to ensure the long-term survival of the world's inhabitants.

Document case study

Fascism: past and future

8.1 A warning from history

There is no rationality in the Nazi hatred: it is a hate that is not in us; it is outside man, it is a poison fruit sprung from the deadly trunk of fascism, but it is outside and beyond fascism itself. We cannot understand it, but we can and must understand from where it springs, and we must be on our guard . . . For this reason, it is everyone's duty to reflect on what happened. Everyone must know, or remember, that when Hitler and Mussolini spoke in public, they were believed, applauded, admired, adored like gods . . . The ideas they proclaimed were not always the same and were, in general, aberrant or silly or cruel. And yet they were acclaimed with hosannas and followed to the death by millions of the faithful . . . Monsters exist, but they are too few in number to be truly dangerous. More dangerous are the common men, the functionaries ready to believe and to act without asking questions, like Eichmann; like Hoess, the commandant of Auschwitz; like Stangl, commandant of Treblinka; like the French military of twenty years later, slaughterers in Algeria; like the Khmer Rouge, of the late seventies, slaughterers in Cambodia . . . A new fascism, with its trail of intolerance, of abuse, and of servitude, can be born outside our country and imported into it, walking on tiptoe and calling itself by other names, or it can loose itself from without with such violence that it routs all defences. At that point, wise counsel no longer serves, and one must find the strength to resist. Even in this contingency, the memory of what happened in the heart of Europe, not very long ago, can serve as a warning and support.

Source: Primo Levi, *If this is a man*, London, 1987, pp. 396–97, quoted in R. Griffin (ed.), *Fascism: a reader*, Oxford, 1995, pp. 391–92

8.2 The true nature of fascism

The way fascism developed during the war passed unnoticed by almost all observers, intent as they were only on condemning it and unconcerned with getting their history right . . . They had been told that fascism was the best bulwark against communism and was also a struggle against the destructiveness of liberalism. But now they know that fascism is a life and death struggle, a desperate last-ditch stand. They know that fascist victory is the only chance to establish a third order, a third world, and the defeat of fascism will condemn men henceforth to know nothing except the sterile confrontation of liberal democracies with communism. They also know that the idea and unity of Europe is not only a propaganda theme: this unity is necessary, it is the only path of salvation between the two monsters that have appeared: and if fascism loses this war, they know that this unity will never be realised, for Europe will be a conquered territory, it will belong either to the United States or Soviet Russia, it will lose its independence and become a new type of colony.

Source: Maurice Bardèche, 'Qu'est-ce que le fascisme?', in Les sept couleurs, Paris, 1961, pp. 175–76, translated by R. Griffin, quoted in R. Griffin (ed.), Fascism: a reader, Oxford, 1995, pp. 320–21

8.3 The 'final order of the European'

Our task is to preserve and to build. If the Fatherland of Europe is lost all is lost. That home of the soul of man must be saved by any sacrifice. First the world of the spirit must unite to resist that final doom of material victory. But beyond lies the grave duty imposed by the new Science. It is not only to build a world worthy of the new genius of man's mind, and secure from the present menace. It is to evoke from the womb of the future a race of men fit to live in that new age. We must deliberately accelerate evolution: it is no longer a matter of volition but of necessity. Is it a sin to strive in union with the revealed purpose of God? . . . From the dust we rise to see a vision that came not before. All things are now possible; and all will be achieved by the final order of the European.

Source: Sir Oswald Mosley, The alternative, Ramsbury, 1947, pp. 313–14

Document case-study questions

1 What does 8.1 tell us about the nature of the 'deadly trunk of fascism'?

2 Why does 8.2 lament the defects of fascism?

3 In what ways does 8.3 connect the 'final order of the European' with the fascist inheritance?

4 What do these sources tell us about the legacy of fascism as seen by fascists and anti-fascists?

Select bibliography

What is fascism?

The most lucid and comprehensive introduction to the subject in both its theoretical and historical dimensions is S. Payne, *A history of fascism, 1914–45*, London, 1995; see also Payne's earlier work, *Fascism: comparison and definition*, Madison, 1980, for how perspectives have altered. Equally rewarding, if more difficult on a conceptual level but displaying an encyclopaedic knowledge of fascism, are R. Griffin, *The nature of fascism*, London, 1991, and R. Griffin, *International fascism*, London, 1998; Griffin's collection of readings and interpretations of fascism provide extensive evidence to support his views, see R. Griffin (ed.), *Fascism: a reader*, Oxford, 1995. The most accessible of the important contributions made by Roger Eatwell are R. Eatwell, *Fascism*, London, 1995, and R. Eatwell, 'Fascism', in R. Eatwell and A. Wright (eds.), *Contemporary political ideologies*, London, 1993. More controversial, but very stimulating, works are Z. Sternhell, *Neither right nor left: fascist ideology in France*, Berkeley, 1986, and Z. Sternhell *et al*, *The birth of fascist ideology*, Princeton, 1994. An excellent, if older, introduction to different aspects of fascism is W. Laqueur (ed.), *Fascism: a reader's guide*, Harmondsworth, 1979. The best, short and well-written Marxist view remains M. Kitchen, *Fascism*, Basingstoke, 1976.

Italian Fascism

The best historical introductions in English to the national context of Italian Fascism remain D. Mack Smith, *Italy*, Ann Arbor, 1959; C. Seton Watson, *Italy from liberalism to Fascism, 1875–1925*, London, 1967; and M. Clark, *Modern Italy, 1871–1982*, London, 1984. On the rise of Fascism, see A. Cardoza, *Agrarian elites and Italian Fascism: the province of Bologna, 1901–26*, Princeton, 1983; P. Corner, *Fascism in Ferrara*, Oxford, 1974; A. Kelikan, *Town and country under Fascism*, Oxford, 1986; F. Snowden, *The Fascist revolution in Tuscany, 1919–22*, Cambridge, 1989; A. Rossi, *The rise of Italian Fascism*, London, 1938; and A. Lyttleton, *The seizure of power: Fascism in Italy, 1919–29*, London, 1973. Of the many books published about Fascist Italy, those especially recommended are D. Mack Smith, *Mussolini*, London, 1981; A. De Grand, *Italian Fascism: its origin and development*, Lincoln, 1989; A. Cassels, *Fascist Italy*, London, 1969; E. Tannenbaum, *Fascism in Italy: society and culture, 1922–45*, London, 1972; T. Koon, *Believe, obey, fight. Socialisation of youth in Fascist Italy*, London, 1985; D. Thompson, *State control in Fascist Italy: culture and conformity, 1925–43*, Manchester, 1991; and J. Whittam, *Fascist Italy*, Manchester, 1995. On Hitler and Mussolini's relationship, the classic account remains F. Deakin, *The brutal friendship*, London, 1962.

Nazism

The literature, in English, on Hitler and Nazism is even more voluminous than that on Mussolini and Fascist Italy. The best introductions to the subject, which give an excellent guide to the literature and controversies, are to be found in I. Kershaw, *The Nazi dictatorship*, 3rd edn, London, 1993, and J. Hiden and J. Farquharson, *Explaining Hitler's Germany*, London, 1989. On Hitler, see I. Kershaw, *Hitler, 1889–1936: hubris*, London, 1998; I. Kershaw, *Hitler, 1936–1945: nemesis*, London, 1999; A. Bullock, *Hitler*, London, 1962; and J. Fest, *Hitler*, London, 1973; for biographical portraits of other Nazi leaders, see J. Fest, *The face of the Third Reich*, Harmondsworth, 1972. For the Nazi economy, see R. Overy, *The Nazi economic recovery, 1932–38*, London, 1982. The best studies of the nature of the Nazi state are M. Broszat, *The Hitler state*, London, 1981; H. Mommsen, *From Weimar to Auschwitz*, London, 1991; and G. Hirschfeld, H. Mommsen and L. Kettenacker (eds.), *The Führer state*, London, 1986. For the impact of Nazism on German society and its destructiveness, see D. Peukert, *Inside Nazi Germany*, London, 1987; I. Kershaw, *The Hitler myth: image and reality in the Third Reich*, Oxford, 1989; T. Childers and J. Caplan (eds.), *Reevaluating the Third Reich*, New York, 1993; M. Burleigh (ed.), *Confronting the Nazi past*, London, 1996; I. Kershaw and M. Lewin (eds.), *Stalinism and Nazism*, Cambridge, 1997; D. F. Crew (ed.), *Nazism and German society, 1933–45*, London, 1994; and M. Burleigh, *Death and deliverance: 'euthanasia' in Germany, 1900–45*, London, 1994. On Nazi racism, anti-Semitism and the Holocaust, see L. Dawidowicz, *The war against the Jews*, New York, 1986; M. Gilbert, *The Holocaust*, London, 1986; C. R. Browning, *The path to genocide*, Cambridge, 1992; M. Burleigh and W. Wipperman, *The racial state: Germany, 1933–45*, Cambridge, 1991; and M. Burleigh, *Ethics and extermination*, Cambridge, 1997.

Other forms of fascism

There are several good collections of essays on inter-war and post-war forms of fascism. These include: S. U. Larsen, B. Hagtvet and J. Myklebust (eds.), *Who were the fascists? Social roots of European fascism*, Bergen, 1980; D. Muhlberger (ed.), *The social basis of fascist movements*, London, 1987; S. Woolf (ed.), *European fascism*, London, 1968; E. Weber, *Varieties of fascism*, London, 1964; and L. Cheles, R. Ferguson and M. Vaughan (eds.), *Neo-fascism in Europe*, London, 1991. Monographs on minor forms of fascism include: M. Conway, *Collaboration in Belgium: Léon Degrelle and the Rexist movement in Belgium, 1940–44*, Oxford, 1994; R. Thurlow, *Fascism in Britain: a history, 1918–85*, Oxford, 1987; N. Talavera, *The Greenshirts and the others*, Stanford, 1970; and G. Harris, *The dark side of Europe*, Edinburgh, 1994.

Chronology

1890–1914 The birth of fascist ideology. The cult of the irrational, heroic vitalism and Enlightenment scientific traditions are influences on the emergence of proto-fascist ideas developed by secondary interpreters of new developments in European thought.

1914–18 The First World War causes the premature deaths of 10 million Europeans, many of them front-line soldiers. The survivors, the 'trenchocracy', as well as 'war socialism' and the role of the state in 'organised capitalism' are all influences on fascism.

1915 The 'radiant days of May', in which the Italian interventionalists, a ragbag coalition from the political extreme right and left, including national syndicalists, nationalists, Futurists, D'Annunzio and Mussolini, agitate for Italian intervention in the First World War.

1917 *October:* the Bolshevik Revolution in Russia leads to the fear of the spread of communism in eastern and central Europe in the aftermath of war.

1917–18 The Romanov, Hohenzollern and Habsburg dynasties of Russia, Germany and Austria-Hungary respectively, collapse.

1918 *9 November:* the end of the First World War. However, the blockade of the Central powers is not lifted until after the signing of the Versailles Treaty in July 1919, thus creating economic, political and social dislocation which encourages the spread of communism.

The creation of the Weimar Republic in Germany following the collapse of the Hohenzollern monarchy.

1919 *January:* the crushing of the Spartacist uprising by the *Freikorps* in Berlin cements the division between reformist and revolutionary socialists.

April: the Soviet Bavarian Republic is overthrown.

1919 Adolf Hitler becomes the fifty-fifth member of Anton Drexler's German Workers' Party (DAP).

March: Benito Mussolini meets the 'Fascists of the first hour' at the Piazza San Sepolcro, Milan, who include interventionists and First World War veterans. The *Partito Nazionale Fascista* (PNF) is formed.

1919–20 Vigilante and paramilitary groups are formed to defend the propertied classes against political collapse and prevent the spread of communism. They include the *Freikorps* (Germany), the *arditi* and *Fascio di Combattimento* (Italy), the *Heimwehr* (Austria) and the Men of Szeged (Hungary).

1920 *April:* the German DAP changes its name to the National Socialist German Workers' Party (NSDAP).

November: Italo Balbo, the fascist *ras* of Ferrara, stages a successful coup against the socialist administration of the city.

December: Dino Grandi, the *ras* of Bologna, overthrows the socialist administration, signalling the spread of the Fascist insurrection to the Po Valley, Tuscany and Apulia.

1921 Hitler becomes leader of the NSDAP.

Mussolini signs a 'pact of pacification' with the socialists. The revolt of the *ras* leads to the temporary resignation of Mussolini.

Giovanni Giolitti brings the Fascists into a national bloc, which gives a spurious air of respectability to the PNF, as well as 38 seats in parliament following the general election.

1922 *October:* following the 'March on Rome', Mussolini becomes prime minister of Italy in a coalition government.

1923 Hyper-inflation in Germany causes the collapse of the mark. French troops occupy the Ruhr region of Germany.

November: the Munich 'Beerhall *Putsch*' ends in a fiasco and Hitler is arrested for high treason.

The PNF and Italian Nationalist Association merge.

1924 *June:* the murder of Giacomo Matteotti sparks a crisis, for which Mussolini takes 'full responsibility'. Mussolini begins to transform the Italian state into a personal dictatorship, a process which lasts until 1929.

Hitler is sentenced to five years in jail for his attempted coup. The National Socialist German Workers' Party (NSDAP) is reorganised as a result of Hitler's determination to follow a constitutional route to power.

1924–29 There is economic and political stability in the Weimar Republic. The Dawes Plan (1924) and Young Plan (1929) scale down the level of Germany's reparation payments.

1929 *February:* the Lateran Treaties are signed, marking Mussolini's success in normalising Church–state relations and obtaining papal recognition of Italy.

October: the Wall Street Crash signals the beginning of the Great Depression and the collapse of the central European banking system from 1930 to 1931. German unemployment levels rise to over 6 million between 1929 and 1932, 33 per cent of the workforce.

1930 *September:* the NSDAP receives 18.3 per cent of the votes in the German general election.

1932 *July:* the NSDAP's votes rise to 37.3 per cent but fall back to 33.1 per cent in November's general election.

October: Oswald Mosley forms the British Union of Fascists (BUF).

1933 *30 January:* Hitler becomes the German chancellor.

February: the Reichstag fire leads to the banning of the German Communist Party, the KPD.

March: the Enabling Act gives Hitler unparalleled executive powers; the neutered Reichstag becomes little more than a rubber-stamping mechanism.

October: Germany leaves the League of Nations and the World Disarmament Conference.

1934 *30 June:* the 'Night of the Long Knives', in which much of the *Sturmabteilung*'s (SA) leadership, including Ernst Röhm, is murdered, along with General Kurt von Schleicher and Gregor Strasser.

July: Chancellor Engelbert Dollfuss is murdered in Austria. Mussolini prevents Germany's *Anschluss* with Austria.

August: the death of President Paul von Hindenburg enables Hitler to unite the posts of chancellor and president and become the *Führer* ('leader') of Germany.

1935 *March:* German rearmament begins as Hitler repudiates the arms-limitation clauses of the Versailles Treaty.

April: Mussolini forms the 'Stresa Front' with Britain and France against German expansionism.

October: Mussolini invades Abyssinia (Ethiopia). The League of Nations imposes sanctions on Italy.

1936 *March:* Hitler's troops march into the Rhineland.

July: the Spanish Civil War begins. Hitler and Mussolini provide men, money, transportation and weapons to enable the eventual victory (in 1939) of Franco's coup against the republican government.

October: the Rome–Berlin Axis is signed; Mussolini is now an ally of Hitler.

24 November: Germany and Japan sign the Anti-Comintern Pact against international communism (which Italy joins on 6 November 1937).

1938 *12–13 March:* Hitler annexes Austria, achieving its *Anschluss* with Germany.

September: the Munich crisis leads to the Munich Agreement. Hitler annexes the Sudetenland by diplomatic means as Chamberlain achieves 'Peace in our time' (or at least until September1939).

9–10 November: Kristallnacht, an anti-Semitic pogrom which signals the acceleration of the discrimination against, and ostracism of, German Jews.

1939 *April:* Italy invades Albania.

May: the 'Pact of Steel' is signed between Hitler and Mussolini, cementing the Fascist–Nazi alliance.

March: Czechoslovakia collapses and much of it is annexed by Hitler.

23 August: the Nazi–Soviet Pact is signed, leading to the partition of Poland.

1 September: Hitler's troops invade Poland.

3 September: Britain and France declare war on Germany. Italy remains a 'non-belligerent'.

1940 *March–June:* the Nazi *Blitzkrieg* rages in western Europe.

May–June: members of the BUF are interned in Britain; the organisation is banned in July.

June: Italy enters the war against the Allies.

1941 *22 June:* Germany begins the invasion of the Soviet Union with Operation Barbarossa.

11 December: Hitler and Mussolini declare war on the United States following the Japanese attack on Pearl Harbor.

1941–42 *December–January:* the Wannsee Conference is held in Berlin, at which the Nazis discuss the extermination of European Jewry in coded language.

1942 *January:* Hitler now controls an empire that stretches from the western seaboard of France to the Ural Mountains and from Norway's North Cape to the Mediterranean Sea.

1942–43 *September–February:* the Battle of Stalingrad, which ends in Germany's eventual surrender, marks a turning point in the war.

1943 *February–July:* the Battle of Kursk; the Red army's victory signals the Soviet break-out into central Europe.

10 July: the Allies begin the invasion of Italy.

20 July: Mussolini is voted out of power.

1943–45 Mussolini is re-established as the Nazi puppet ruler of the Italian Social Republic (Republic of Salò) in northern Italy.

1944 *July:* Allied forces invade Normandy. Britain, the USA and France establish a second front in France.

1945 *28 April:* Mussolini and his mistress are shot by Italian partisans and hung upside down from a garage roof in Milan.

30 April: Hitler (and Goebbels) commit suicide in a bunker in Berlin.

8 May: Nazi Germany surrenders unconditionally to the Allies.

1946 The Nuremberg Trials are held and the surviving Nazi leaders are punished.

1947 The onset of the Cold War signals the lessening importance of the pursuit of former Fascists and Nazis. Small revivals, in altered form, of types of neo-fascism, radical-right and racial-populist organisations begin.

Glossary

Action Française: formed in 1899, the *Action Française* was a reactionary, monarchist, anti-Semitic and anti-Dreyfus literary circle, organised around the newspaper *Action Française* and its editor Charles Maurras. It organised a bodyguard, the *Camelots du Roi*, to protect its premises and was involved in the *Cercle Proudhon*, the meetings of national syndicalists and monarchists which acted as a precursor of fascism between 1911 and 1913. It supported the Vichy regime between 1940 and 1944.

Arrow Cross Party (*Nyilaskereszt*): green-shirted Hungarian fascists led by Ferenc Szálasi. It seized power momentarily in October 1944 and its members were enthusiastic collaborators in the Nazi destruction of Hungarian Jewry.

Barbarossa, Operation: the Nazi codename for the German invasion of the Soviet Union, 1941–45.

British Fascisti (later renamed British Fascists): the first British fascist movement, 1923–35, led by Rotha Lintorn-Orman.

British Union of Fascists (BUF): created and led by Sir Oswald Mosley from 1932 to 1940, the BUF was the most significant British fascist party, with 40–50,000 members in July 1934.

Codreanu, Corneliu: the leader of Romanian fascism who founded the Legion of the Archangel Michael and the Iron Guard. He was shot by government agents 'while trying to escape' from prison in 1938.

Croix de Feu (later the *Parti Social Français*): the 'Cross of Fire' was a French radical-right/neo-fascist movement led by Colonel François de la Rocque. It was reputed to have 600,000 members when it was banned in 1936.

Degrelle, Léon: leader of the Belgian Rexist Party, 1936–45, which began as an extreme-right, Catholic, nationalist movement and became a pro-Nazi collaborator during the war. Degrelle won a Nazi medal on the Eastern Front fighting the Soviet Union and was one of the organisers of the international Charlemagne Division of the SS. Although sentenced to death in his absence in 1945, he escaped to Spain and lived until the 1990s.

Le Faisceau: 'The Fasces' was a French fascist party led by George Valois from 1925 to 1927.

Falange: the authentic Spanish fascist party from 1933 to 1936, its 'shotgun marriage' with the other political elements of the nationalist rebellion in 1936 turned it into Franco's 'poodle' as the official governing party and mouthpiece of the reactionary right.

fascism: general (or generic features) common to national movements. A fascist movement or ideology was usually based on the leadership principle and incorporated beliefs in revolutionary nationalism advocated by a mass movement which desired the creation of a 'new order'. It fundamentally represented an 'alternative revolution', which was radically opposed to socialism, communism, bourgeois democracy and authoritarianism based on traditional elites. The term 'fascism' derives from the Italian word *fascio*, meaning 'band', 'union' or 'league', which had traditionally been used to  describe left-wing populist movements before Mussolini's hijacking of the term. The word *fascio* is derived from the Latin *fasces*, which referred both to a bundle of sticks with protruding axeheads tied together and a symbol of authority which was carried by a minor Roman official who preceded magistrates in the streets of ancient Rome. The rods represented punishment; the axeheads, execution.

Fascists: members of the Italian Fascist Party (*Partito Nazionale Fascista*, PNF), which was created and led by Mussolini between 1919 and 1945.

'fifth column': the mainly mythical domestic (fascist) collaborators who allegedly undermined national resistance to the Nazis in 1940 and were often used as scapegoats to explain Hitler's rapid victories. The expression was first used by a Spanish general when four columns were advancing on Madrid in the Spanish Civil War. The 'fifth column' were fascist sympathisers inside the city.

Franco, Francisco: Franco became the leader of the successful nationalist rebellion which led to the Spanish Civil War, 1936–39, by default. He had the considerable help of Hitler and Mussolini. *El Caudillo* ('the leader'), he was, in effect, the Spanish dictator from 1939 until his death in 1975.

Gestapo (*Geheime Staatspolizei*): the secret police of the Nazi state. Its much-vaunted efficiency was a political myth.

Gleichschaltung: the 'co-ordination' of state and society in the Nazi system of government.

Goebbels, Joseph: the Nazi minister of propaganda from 1933 to 1945.

Göring, Hermann: the Nazi head of the *Luftwaffe* (military air-force) who was also in charge of the Four-year Plan. The 'iron man' was the second most powerful Nazi leader during the 1930s.

Himmler, Heinrich: the Nazi head of the *Schutzstaffel* (SS) and police in the Nazi state.

Hitler, Adolf: the chancellor of Germany from 1933 to 1945 who combined the position with the role of president after the death of von Hindenburg in 1934 to wield, in theory, almost absolute power in the Nazi state as *Führer* ('leader').

Interventionists: an informal political alliance of elements from the extreme left and right (including Mussolini, the national syndicalists, the Italian Nationalist Association, the Futurists and Gabriele D'Annunzio) which demanded Italian intervention in the First World War. Most of these elements would be re-formed as the 'fascists of the first hour' at the Piazza San Sepolcro, Milan, in March 1919.

Iron Guard: the main Romanian fascist movement, which was formed in 1930 and led by Corneliu Codreanu, it became one of the most significant fascist movements outside Italy and Germany. Virulently anti-Semitic, the Iron Guard was noted for its mystical fascism and racial nationalism.

Italian Social Republic: sarcastically referred to as the 'Republic of Salò', the regime which Mussolini governed as Hitler's puppet ruler of northern Italy between 1943 and 1945.

Kristallnacht ('crystal night'): an anti-Jewish pogrom which occurred on the night of 9–10 November 1938, allegedly a reprisal for the murder of a German diplomat in Paris by a Jewish student.

Legion of the Archangel Michael: formed in 1927, a Romanian secret society that was noted for its violence and for training the cadre of Romanian fascist leaders. Codreanu formed it as a result of instructions that were allegedly given to him in a dream by the Archangel Michael. The Iron Guard developed from the legion.

Matteotti crisis: the murder of the socialist deputy, Giacomo Matteotti (which was indirectly instigated by Mussolini), in 1924 and the failure during the subsequent crisis to challenge Fascist rule led to Mussolini acquiring greatly enhanced personal power.

Mosley, Oswald: the leader of the British Union of Fascists (BUF) from 1932 to 1940 and founder of the Union Movement in 1948.

Mussolini, Benito: *Il Duce* ('the leader'), the founder and leader of Italian Fascism from 1919 to 1945. A former revolutionary socialist, he was the Italian prime minister from 1922 to 1943 and head of the Nazi puppet state, the Italian Social Republic, from 1943 to 1945.

Nazis: members of the National Socialist German Workers' Party (*Nationalsozialistische Deutsche Arbeiterpartei*, NSDAP), founded in 1919 by Anton Drexler as the German Workers' Party (*Deutsche Arbeiterpartei*, DAP), and led by the *Führer*, Adolf Hitler, from 1919 to 1945.

'Night of the Long Knives': on 30 June 1934 Ernst Röhm and much of the *Sturmabteilung*'s (SA) leadership, as well as General Kurt von Schleicher and Gregor Strasser, were murdered on the orders of Hitler, thus simultaneously reassuring the *Reichswehr*, settling political scores and instigating the rise of the SS.

Nuremberg Trials: post-war trials at which justice was meted out to the surviving Nazi leaders by the Allies in 1946.

OVRA: the special political police of the Italian Ministry of the Interior established by Mussolini.

Quisling, Vidkun: the leader of the *Nasjonal Samling* (National Unification) Party, the Norwegian national socialist party. His name became synonymous with treachery and collaboration in most European languages during the Second World War.

Parti Populaire Français **(PPF):** a party formed by the former communist Jacques Doriot in 1936. Although he denied being a fascist, members of the PPF were amongst the leading collaborators with the Nazis during the Second World War.

ras: the regional leaders, such as Italo Balbo (Ferrara), Dino Grandi (Bologna), Roberto Farinacci (Cremona) and Filippo Turati (Brescia), of Italian Fascism.

Reichswehr: the German army, renamed *Wehrmacht* during the Second World War.

Salazar, António de Oliveira: the Portuguese dictator from 1934 to 1971.

syndicalism: a form of socialism based on the theory of the ownership and control of industry directly by the workers rather than ownership and control by the state. Syndicalists aimed to further workers' interests by direct action through strikes and industrial sabotage.

'White Guards': a useful Marxist term for the groups of demobilised former soldiers who became proto-fascist, counter-revolutionary opponents to the Bolshevik Revolution in the aftermath of the First World War. The term includes such groups as the *Freikorps* (Germany), the *arditi* and *Fascio di Combattimento* (Italy), the *Heimwehr* (Austria) and the Men of Szeged (Hungary).

Index

Abyssinia, Italian invasion of (1935), 32, 33, 34, 58, 73
Almirante, Giorgio, 94
'alternative revolution' of fascism, 6–9, 62, 66; and Nazism, 6–7, 9, 43
Anti-Comintern Pact, 34
anti-fascism, 71–80, 91
anti-immigrant movements, 97–8, 99
anti-Semitism, 97; and fascist ideologies, 64–5; in the German states, 13; and Italian Fascism, 1, 34–5, 58; and Nazism, 1, 6–7, 35, 40, 54, 55, 56, 57; *see also* Jews
Antonescu, Ion, 17, 68, 78
Arendt, Hannah, 4
Austria, 66, 76, 79, 83
Austrian Freedom Party, 98

Bebel, August, 40
Belgian Rexist Party, 65, 69, 83, 85
Benoist, Alain de, 96
Bolshevik Revolution: and the anti-fascist movement, 72, 74; and Nazism, 60; and the origins of fascism, 3, 6, 12, 16, 17, 18
Britain: Communist Party (CPGB), 75, 79–80; Imperial Fascist League, 98; Labour Party, 75; and the Second World War, 82; and the Spanish Civil War, 77, 78, 79
British Fascisti, 63
British National Party, 98
British Union of Fascists (BUF), 2, 9, 35, 65, 66, 67, 69, 108
Brüning, Heinrich, 42, 43, 45

capitalism: and fascism, 2, 3, 4, 6, 18, 19; and the First World War, 15
Catholic Church: and Franco's Spain, 66, 77–8; and Italian Fascism, 27, 29; and the Italian state, 23, 24, 29; and Nazism, 46–7
Cavour, Count, 23
class-based theory of fascism, 3–4
Codreanu, Corneliu, 17, 64, 68, 70, 108
Cold War, 91, 92, 93–4
collective security, failure of, 75–6, 79
Comintern (the Communist International), 34, 72, 73, 74–5, 79
communism: and the anti-fascist movement, 72, 73, 74–5; and the Cold War, 93; and fascism, 2, 4, 6, 16, 17, 18, 19, 66; and Italian Fascism, 27, 28, 34; and the Spanish Civil War, 76, 77

'conservative revolutionaries', 96
corporatism, and Italian Fascism, 33

D'Annunzio, Gabriele, 22, 30
Degrelle, Léon, 83, 84, 108
Dimitrov, Georgi, 74–5, 79

Eastern Europe: failure of fascism in, 17, 19; fascism and ethnicity in, 98–9; fascist movements in, 64–5, 66; and the Second World War, 86–9, 99
Eatwell, Roger, 5–6
Ebert, Friedrich, 41
Enlightenment ideology, and the origins of fascism, 5, 12, 13
'Euro-fascist' movements, 96
European fascism, 62–70; and Nazism, 83–4
European Union (EU), 97, 98, 99
Evola, Julius, 96
'extremism of the centre', fascism as, 3–4

failure of fascism, 19, 62; reasons for, 67–8
Fascist Italy, *see* Italian Fascism
Federzoni, Luigi, 29
Fichte, Johann Gottlieb, 13
First World War: and Italian Fascism, 22, 23–4; and Nazism, 39–41; and the origins of fascism, 3, 12, 15–16, 18–19, 20, 62
France: *Action Française*, 5, 63, 108; anti-immigration party (*Front National*), 96, 98, 99; fascist ideology in, 68, 84–5; fascist movements in, 6, 63–4, 65, 66, 108; popular-front government in, 72, 75, 78; and Spanish Civil War, 77, 78–9; Vichy regime, 85, 86
Franco, General Francisco, 35, 64, 66–7, 76, 77–8, 86, 95, 109
French Revolution, and the origins of fascism, 5, 12, 14–15, 18
Freud, Sigmund, 14
Friedrich, Carl, 4
future of fascism, 99–100
Futurist movement, 22, 30

Garibaldi, Giuseppe, 23
generic concept of fascism, 2–4, 10
Germany: anti-fascist movement in, 72, 74; anti-immigrant movements in, 98, 99; economy, 41–3, 45, 51–2, 59–60; and the

Printed in the United States
By Bookmasters